> "I do believe something magical can happen when you read a good book"
> -J.K. Rowling

Author of the Harry Potter book series

This book is a gift

To

From

Enjoy and Share

WIDE OPEN

THE TEN EYES OF LEADERSHIP

Michael Kouly

Copyright © 2017 by Michael Kouly

All rights reserved

No part of this publication may be reproduced, distributed, or transmitted in any form or by any means, including photocopying, recording, or other electronic or mechanical methods, without the prior written permission of the publisher, except in the case of brief quotations embodied in critical reviews and certain other noncommercial uses permitted by copyright law.

First Edition

ISBN 978-0-9992181-2-9

To my

Wife Sandra   *Father Mgr. Paul*   *Mother Helen*

CONTENTS

Preface		*viii*
Acknowledgements		*xi*
Whose Eyes are These?		*xii*
Introduction		14
1.	The Five Pillars	26
2.	The First Eye: Self-Awareness	49
3.	The Second Eye: What Matters Most	101
4.	The Third Eye: Purpose	115
5.	The Fourth Eye: Understanding Others	143

6.	The Fifth Eye: How Others Perceive You	161
7.	The Sixth Eye: The Unsaid	187
8.	The Seventh Eye: Systems	206
9.	The Eighth Eye: Enemies	226
10.	The Ninth Eye: The Unexpected	259
11.	The Tenth Eye: Authority	281
12.	The Technology of Leadership	310
13.	Keep Your Eyes Wide Open	313

Notes   316

About The author   321

PREFACE

I have spent my life observing, thinking about, and researching leadership. Even as a child, I was very intrigued by leadership; it captured my attention like nothing else. In my sixteen years as a journalist for Reuters Middle East, I observed leadership in the numerous people and events I wrote about — in fields ranging from war to business to affairs of state.

As I advanced in my career with Reuters, I was exposed to the inner workings of a large multinational organization, receiving an opportunity to put my thoughts about leadership to the test as Managing Director for Reuters Middle East and, ultimately, as an executive board member for Reuters Continental Europe, Middle East, and Africa.

Subsequently, I took a leave from business to further pursue my interest in leadership from an academic perspective, studying with some of the great minds in the field at such institutions as Princeton, Harvard's Kennedy School of Government, Harvard Business School, and others.

I was later lured back into the business world, and my fascination with the subject of leadership increased. I participated in a variety of workshops and created an intensive four-day Executive Leadership Program, which I have presented over the past twelve years. All of which put me in contact with thousands of managers and CEOs from countries all over the world. These workshops and programs, or "Leadership Simulations" as I call them, have been among the most insightful and moving experiences of my life. I have learned so much from each and every individual who has shared life and leadership experiences with me through these various programs, workshops, and simulations.

As a result of my observations and reflections on what I learned through these years, I developed a personal philosophy of life and leadership that has served me well. I believe this philosophy is crucial for the survival and growth of any individual, organization and, indeed, society, which is why I decided to share it in this book.

This book is about seeing the world differently, or perhaps seeing it for the first time. It is about shedding awareness on essential parts of leadership and the 10 eyes that need to be opened to begin exercising leadership. In that regard, I have adopted a metaphor from the character Argus Panoptes, the giant from Greek mythology with a hundred eyes. His name, Panoptes, means "the all-seeing." He was a very effective watchman because only a few of his eyes would sleep at one time, while the remaining eyes always stayed awake and constantly watching.

While it may be interesting (and slightly overwhelming) to see the world simultaneously through a hundred eyes, I am going to discuss just ten "eyes" of leadership. These eyes are ten kinds of awareness and perception which can make you, if not all-seeing, at least an excellent watchman, and therefore a well-prepared leader. This book covers the ten metaphorical eyes of leadership which are grounded in five main pillars, and which must always be awake and constantly watching. This book is about using the awareness you will discover from developing these ten eyes to exercise leadership and create positive change in the world. So, let's begin...

ACKNOWLEDGEMENTS

This book was possible because of the gracious contributions of several beautiful people.

I would like to acknowledge my colleagues: Sandra Chaoul, Marwa Itani, Sara Mansour and Najwa Ghotmi who spent months translating my thoughts into the paragraphs that you are about to read. Mary Shammas, who designed and formatted the book for printing. Karen Tallentire and Douglas Williams, who helped with editing and Roy Sayegh with proofreading.

Special thanks to: Bill Starnes, who reviewed the book several times and offered invaluable ideas that enhanced the content. Metta Murdaya, Mohammed Al-Ayouti, and Paulette Pidcock who offered insightful feedback and suggestions that enhanced the reading experience. Susan Simons who provided elegant thoughts on the design and the production of the book.

A heartfelt thanks to my wife, Sandra, for being an inspiring example of a hero's journey of survival and growth and to my father, Mgr. Paul Kouly, and mother, Helen Kouly, for being the blessing that raised a family of beautiful people who appreciate life, love and leadership.

Finally, I would like to thank you, honorable reader, for your trust and for the time you will spend reading the book. I would love to read your comments, reviews, and thoughts on how to further enhance the message of this book.

Whose eyes are these?

Dear Reader,

The Eye Portraits that you will see inside the book belong to well-known people who made, or are still making, a difference in their communities. I have included these leaders because each is an exceptional example of the brilliant use of one or more of the 10 Eyes that are mentioned in the book.

It would be fun to figure out to whom these eyes belong? Which of the 10 Eyes did they use particularly well? The purpose is to learn, in an entertaining way, from the example of such remarkable people so that we become better at exercising leadership in the ultimate journey of survival and growth.

To offer you a helping hand, I have included a list (on the next page) of 52 well-known people. You can use this to help you figure out whose eyes each Eye Portrait belongs to. Visit www.koulyinstitute.com/book/eyes and send me an email with your answers; I will let you know how many you guessed correctly.

Enjoy the exciting and amusing adventure of discovering these outstanding people and share with us your thoughts, comments, reviews, and suggestions by visiting our website: **koulyinstitute.com** or emailing us at **books@michaelkouly.com**

Have fun!

Abraham Lincoln	Hilary Clinton	Mother Teresa
Albert Einstein	Indira Gandhi	Nelson Mandela
Albert Schweitzer	J.K. Rowling	Oprah Winfrey
Angela Merkel	J.R.R. Tolkien	Oscar Wilde
Angelina Jolie	Jack Ma	Pablo Picasso
Anne Frank	Jawaharlal Nehru	Pele
Barack Obama	Kofi Annan	Pope John Paul II
Benazir Bhutto	Lee Kuan Yew	Princess Diana
Bill Clinton	Leo Tolstoy	Queen Elizabeth II
Bill Gates	Mahatma Gandhi	Richard Branson
Billie Jean King	Malala Yousafzai	Rosa Parks
Charles de Gaulle	Malcolm X	Sheikh Mohammed Bin Rashid Al Maktoum
Dalai Lama	Margaret Thatcher	
Desmond Tutu	Marie Curie	Virginia Woolf
Eva Peron	Martin Luther King Jr.	Vladimir Putin
Fidel Castro		Winston Churchill
Florence Nightingale	Mikhail Gorbachev	Xi Jinping
Franklin D. Roosevelt	Mohammed Ali	
	Mohammed Ali Jinnah	

INTRODUCTION

"The world is full of magic things, patiently waiting for our senses to grow sharper."

-W.B. YEATS

What Keeps You Alive?

Imagine this: You're blind. You're deaf. And you're walking in a minefield. What is the likelihood that you will come out alive? It doesn't look good, right?

Though it may come as a surprise to many, this scenario is not as unlikely as it may seem. But in a more figurative sense, the triggering of a full-blown mine blast is not limited, unfortunately, to a deficiency in our senses or an actual war zone. Figurative mine blasts can result from lack of perception in our daily lives.

Our everyday world can be like a minefield when we fail to notice the warning signs all around us. The signals can come in many forms, whether from the inside (our thoughts, emotions, and physical reactions) or our external surroundings (the environment and our relations with others). As an old saying puts it, "Although we are not blind, we often do not see; and although we are not deaf, we often do not hear or understand." This lack of perception causes us to miss valuable information that impacts the way we, and others, live and progress.

Staying alive requires gathering as much information from our surroundings as we can, and using it intelligently. Our physical, emotional, professional, and social survival is at stake if we fail to develop an ongoing awareness of ourselves and of the systems that we are part of (e.g. family, organization, society, country and world).

> **Staying alive requires gathering and understanding as much information as you can from the world around you; this is even truer when exercising leadership.**

Leadership is such a heavy word. Yet most people take it lightly. Did you know that if you Google "leadership" you will get almost half a billion hits? Did you know there are more than fifteen hundred definitions of leadership, various leadership styles, and numerous views of what a true leader is? Examples of these views include, "The leader always sets a trail for others to follow." Or, "A leader knows more than others and sees better than others." Adjectives are being thrown out right and left to describe leaders and leadership. There is the spiritual leader, the servant leader, the quiet leader, the design leader, the strategic leader. Blah, blah, blah...

I don't know about you, but I am fed up — up to my big nose! The world has squeezed every last aspect of leadership and placed levels, sublevels, and different branches under it. This unnecessary division has complicated the meaning of leadership and made it the equivalent of a 'lost-in-translation' moment. There are so many definitions of what a leader is, and what acts of leadership are, that the core meaning is lost.

If you agree with the slogans above, well then, we have a lot of work to do. Gathering followers and standing out is not what leadership is about. It is not about fame and being in the spotlight. It is not about knowing more than others and being the smartest person in the room. And it is not about power or being in a position of authority. Therefore, I suggest, at least while reading this book, that you forget the typical definitions of a leader, even if for a while, and explore possibilities of rethinking about this important term.

If we want to capture what true leadership is about, we need to understand this fundamental question: *Why is leadership necessary?*

In today's world, we have so many stimuli and media outlets that people get lost in the layers of accumulated nonsense. To reach the core of anything you must clear away the dust and bullshit. Sometimes the best way to truly understand something is to go back to its origins. So, why was leadership originally needed? It was to make sure that life progressed and advanced. It was to support the ultimate purpose of life: survival and growth.

Everything, whether a single-celled organism, a plant, an animal, a human, or even an organization or country, wants two things: to survive (remain sustainable) and to grow (gain knowledge and expand). These two concepts are universal in their meaning, although their expression varies from one organism to another. For ants, it is merely to gather enough food to sustain their colony. For the lion, it is to assert power over the pride and to remain in power for as long as he can. For humans, it gets a little bit more complicated.

You can think of it as follows: Humans require peace to survive, because without peace, we have war or other calamities such as famine, and people die. But for humans, unlike our animal counterparts, surviving is just not enough. We have reached a point where our basic needs can be met very easily (for most people at least). Humans no longer must hunt to survive; they can just pick up a phone, place an order, request a delivery, and the food comes to them. We have adapted the world around our needs so that we no longer spend our days just trying to survive or worrying about threats from the outside.

Why is it then that you still have individuals committing suicide in countries such as Sweden, a prime example of a safe country where the people are provided with everything they need to maintain their rights and assure their survival? Survival is not enough anymore. As humans, we need the second part of the ultimate purpose, which is growth, and it is as essential as survival. Only with growth, discovery, and knowledge can we attain joy and fulfillment.

For humans to fulfill this ultimate purpose, they must feel positive emotions (such as hope, joy and happiness) or undergo positive experiences. Otherwise, they will either live an unfulfilled, sad life or take sadness to the extreme and they will not want to live anymore. When people are fulfilled, they are more productive and tolerant; it is easier for them to exercise leadership through interventions, and the interventions are more successful. When people are unfulfilled, unhappiness affects their health, their longevity, and the work they do. Fulfillment injects meaning into everyday actions; without it, individuals would be drones, zombies, living each day just to get by. Life without fulfillment would be survival without the growth.

Humans require happiness and fulfillment. They yearn for a dignified life lived in peace and joy, where they feel alive and can continue to prosper. The Universal Declaration of Human Rights, along with other forms of understanding the world around us such as religion and science, all seem to agree on this point. Through survival and growth, the world gets better and we move forward.

> *"All religions, arts and sciences are branches of the same tree. They are all directed toward ENNOBLING MAN'S LIFE and LIFTING IT from the sphere of mere physical existence ."*
>
> -ALBERT EINSTEIN

The problem today is that most people are not focused on growth; they are focused on merely surviving (e.g. economically, socially or professionally) and consequently living with all the substantial stress that comes along with that. Many people just go through the day from one distraction to another. After they go to work, instead of socializing and connecting with others, they will sit almost zombie-like in front of a TV screen. They spend eight- to nine-hour days in jobs they find draining or revolting, just to pay off their mounting bills, taxes, and mortgages. Instead of being present in the moment and dealing with reality, they take drugs and drink excessive amounts of alcohol to deal with their problems and numb the pain. It is almost as if in today's world we are trying to run away from life instead of actually living and fulfilling our amazing potential as human beings.

Society, the world, is stuck. We are stuck. The evidence is clear when individuals would rather become highly medicated, overly distracted, and addicted to social media than confront problems or issues. We are living in a virtual reality — no, not living, not really.

We need acts of leadership to get people to move forward, and that doesn't mean we wait around for a leader to arise. We need acts of leadership in our own lives to get ourselves on the right path. It is hard for people who are trapped and avoidant to move forward, let alone thrive. An organization, group, or person that is trapped cannot contribute much to survival and growth. Acts of leadership are about moving individuals, groups, and organizations forward, getting them unstuck or helping them capture opportunities so they can achieve purposeful success and create a better reality.

So, the fundamental questions to ask are, **"How alive are you? What is the quality of your experience of life? Are you fulfilled? Are you growing? Or are you running away and distracting yourself?"**

My philosophy of leadership is as follows. There is no such thing as a Leader in the sense of how it is commonly defined; there are only acts of leadership. A leader in the conventional sense, or an individual with a formal position, is what I define as an "authority figure": a boss, CEO, father, mother, teacher, etc. Authority is a position in the hierarchy that can be labeled, a position of formal power. All organizational titles represent a position in the hierarchy, and hence can be considered positions of authority.

Leadership is something different; it lies not in a particular position, but in an act or intervention to mobilize individuals to successfully capture opportunities so they can move forward to survive and grow. While you are exercising leadership — at that moment — you would be considered a leader.

Note that one need not have a title or be in a formal position of authority to exercise leadership. That being said, when one does exercise leadership effectively, one typically gains informal authority in the moment as a result. (Such informal authority also would accrue to those with formal authority who exercise true leadership, further cementing their position as an authority figure). Continued effectiveness through acts of leadership may result in sufficient informal authority, that the individual exercising leadership may be offered a position of formal authority within the group.

Even without a formal title, one's consistent leadership can accumulate to the point of being acknowledged as a leader on a global scale. Consider such individuals as Mahatma Gandhi and Mother Teresa who, despite having no formal authority, were considered leaders of their time. Hence, with the right skill set and motivating purpose, anyone can exercise leadership; leadership does not have to be exercised by an authority figure to work. Although being in a position of power makes it easier to exercise leadership, a position is not a necessity.

What is imperative is the right amount of awareness coming from the ten eyes I will introduce. It is not about standing out and leading the pack. Leadership is about continually understanding the purpose (that is why you need awareness) of whatever group or individual you are trying to help grow, and getting the group or individual to move toward that purpose. Leaders do not need to know everything; leaders just need to be aware of the situation and be focused on the purpose so they can mobilize people toward a better reality.

For example, when six people are in a room arguing, nobody is hearing anyone. The individual who somehow can redirect their attention to a more productive and efficient form of communication would have exercised leadership. Let's go even further. Suppose someone is walking on the street and notices trash on the ground. If this person starts to pick up the trash and throw it in the garbage and a child observes the act and starts to help out, what the person did would be an act of leadership. Anything that helps mobilize support and gets individuals or groups moving forward towards a greater purpose is an act of leadership.

Leadership is not easy, and many times groups and people (all a part of systems) will resist painful change. Systems have behaviors and patterns that have lasted a long time simply because these behaviors have obvious and underlying benefits that maintain the equilibrium of the group. Sometimes even if a change would otherwise benefit the whole group, the system will still resist, making the task of leadership even harder. This is due to the fact that the system is stuck in its default behaviors and comfort zone and does not have the maturity to tolerate pain or discomfort for the sake of progress. Hence, for leaders to interrupt or shake the default settings of the system, they must have the courage to face opposition.

Acts of leadership require persistence, and even more importantly, require care and compassion, because only with care and compassion will you have the strength to weather any storm as you mobilize others. This need for persistence is seen in companies where the management is corrupt or stealing money. If any person wants to exercise leadership and promote transparency, the other individuals who are getting rich from the corruption will be plotting against the person who is bold enough to shake the system. Leadership is just a process, a mechanism, but no one said it was easy.

Let me be clear. Although leadership has been a longtime passion of mine, and I have spent thousands of hours teaching and practicing it, this is not a conventional book about leadership. It will not delve into the dos and don'ts of leadership, strategies, etc… This is a book about something more important and more fundamental, something that is absolutely necessary for you as you exercise leadership. This book is about staying alive and interpreting your environment.

Why is this so important? Because most acts of leadership fail and sometimes those who exercise them get marginalized, not for lack of intelligence or intellect, but for not paying attention to the fundamentals. I have heard numerous stories of how ignoring the fundamentals made world-renowned experts in leadership thinking fail in their acts of leadership. Also, how presidents of countries have lost their positions because of not paying attention to the basics.

Everyone loses if you are neutralized, marginalized, or kicked out. The challenge is to stay in the system and work within it to mobilize the system toward progress. You cannot do that unless you are alive physically, professionally, socially, and politically.

Just to clarify another viewpoint, leadership is about hope

even in a state of despair. It is about spreading optimism and uplifting spirits. This book, I warn you, may make you feel a little on alert (on purpose) because the context of leadership is messy, chaotic, uncertain, confusing, and dangerous. Think of it this way, before someone becomes an elite special forces officer specialized in operating covertly in enemy territory, they must master the skills involved with survival techniques; before one is trained in firefighting, they undergo a rigorous training aimed at techniques that will shield them and help them put out a fire in the fastest way possible. Leadership involves purposefully pushing and being pushed back upon, purposefully provoking conflicts and managing them — basically operating in the eye of the storm. That kind of action definitely requires survival skills.

Leadership requires awareness. Awareness is vital; with every step you take, you must be aware of the effect it has on all those around you. The knowledge that leadership requires rests on five basic pillars that we have called "The Kouly Model for Survival and Growth". These pillars are the foundation for survival and growth. They keep us present in the moment and aware of ourselves, of others, and of the organizations or systems of which we are a part. These pillars also support our awareness of the role of authority in those systems as well as the leadership skills needed to act on your awareness to mobilize others towards further survival and growth.

From the vantage points atop these pillars, your ten eyes, once fully developed and activated, can survey your environment, discerning clues and signals that support your acts of leadership. Until we have a firm understanding of these pillars and the tools to erect them, we cannot truly and effectively exercise the kind of leadership that helps individuals and systems survive and thrive .

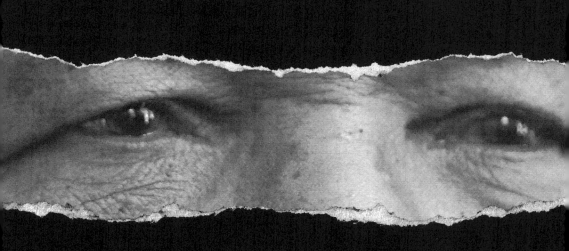

Whose eyes are these?

THE KOULY MODEL

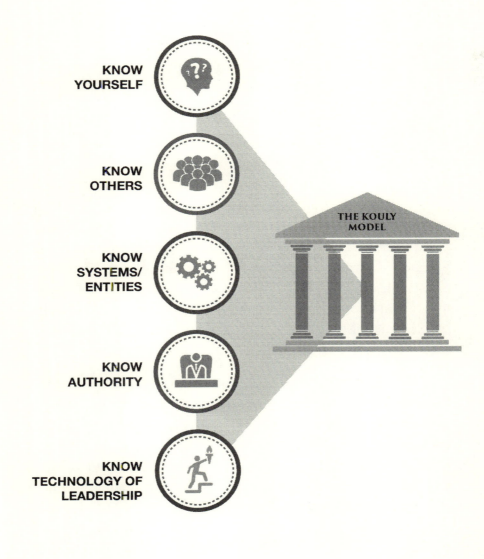

CHAPTER ONE

THE FIVE PILLARS

A few years back, when I was first starting the Cambridge Institute for Global Leadership, I met a man who taught me just how dangerous exercising leadership can be. When exercising leadership, it is imperative for you to be constantly aware and have all your eyes open. He was a former President who started off with a vision to aid his country, but ended in exile. How did this happen?

His presidency lasted less than two years before he had hundreds of people protesting and plotting a military coup. He became president during one of the hardest times for his country, as it was slowly plunging into an economic depression. He was so eager to solve the problems quickly and swiftly that he did not realize how he may have alienated various individuals and factions.

Leadership often is about turning up the heat and making

needed changes, but it is important not to tip the entire boat before you start moving forward. His introduction of too many changes all at once overwhelmed the entire system of governance he was trying to protect. To reduce the country's financial debt, he got rid of subsidies for gas and electricity, resulting in prices skyrocketing for civilians. In doing this, he neglected to sufficiently consider how this would aggravate the citizens, who already were suffering from the financial situation and high rates of unemployment.

In a last attempt to solve the country's economic problems, he wanted to switch the country's currency to the U.S. dollar, which was also met with great resistance. He was so eager to get results that he did not realize he needed to look deeper and take it one step at a time; for example, focusing on the banking systems and strengthening them. Acts of leadership take time and, especially when you are in the direst of situations, your eyes must be open. This is why understanding the five pillars is imperative. Things may have ended very differently had this president been aware of how others would respond to his initiatives, the behind-the-scenes plots, and the great dissatisfaction his policies would create.

He also underestimated his enemies and for that he was forced to flee the country he had sworn to protect. When your eyes are closed to everything except a specific goal you want to achieve, you may lose sight of other important factors. For example, it is important to recognize your own agendas and needs. This president may have had selfless intentions or perhaps he was too eager to make a good name for himself and create his legacy, allowing his ego to lead the way. These intentions factor into why he made the decisions he did.

When exercising leadership, it is important to ask yourself

if your intentions are for the good of the whole, or self-serving. Even when it seems like there are no other options, sometimes small changes that are sustainable can be just as powerful as large ones. But it is about being aware of what the people around you need to move toward a better life at a rate they can tolerate. Leadership is about moving, if possible, the entire system or group forward, so all your own personal agendas or biases must be pushed aside in order to cater to the whole.

This is not to say that this man's presidency was an utter failure. In fact, his ability to strike a peace treaty with a neighboring country that for many years shared hostility with his own, had been a step toward progress. But each step takes time, and each has its own form of resistance. That is why it is essential to keep your eyes wide open. He underestimated his enemies, he was too enthusiastic about solving problems, and he was making decisions without accurately assessing the cost to others. It was not that his credentials were short. Sometimes even with a large library of knowledge, nothing can compare to awareness that comes from understanding oneself, others, the system, and authority, all of which are key factors to take into consideration when exercising leadership.

The Five Pillars

Imagine that you are standing in the Parthenon, surrounded by pillars supporting this magnificent structure. Try to imagine what would happen if one pillar were to fall or break. Leadership, in a similar sense, is held together by five main pillars: Know yourself, know others, know systems, know authority, and know the technology of leadership (skills). The first four can be seen as the base of the temple and the only way for the fifth to arise is if the first four are sturdy enough to carry it.

These five pillars are a holistic view of the ecosystem of our lives. No matter what the situation, your life will be affected by at least one or two of these pillars, if not all. You need to understand how to get all these elements to work together in a functional manner, and the fifth pillar is essential because it pulls each of the others together and aids in their interaction.

In the next few pages, you will be introduced to the five pillars, which are the fundamentals of exercising leadership and will help you survive the process. Without these, even the most knowledgeable of individuals will fall short. Furthermore, each pillar includes a tool or various 'eyes' that need to be opened to get the best results.

THE
TEN EYES
OF LEADERSHIP

Pillar One — Know Yourself

She was someone who could be considered self-centered. Whenever she was in a relationship, she expected too much too quickly, and when she did not get what she wanted, she would vocalize it loudly. Her friendships would entail her complaining about her life, her other relationships, and, if she was not the center of attention, she would get upset. Slowly, people started to move away from her. It even affected her work life, as her colleagues could not stand to be around her for long periods of time, and the promotion for a senior executive position that she wanted never came through. She was supposed to oversee a group at work, but due to her lack of awareness of herself, she never could command the respect of her colleagues. Her best friend, or at least the person she thought was her best friend, considered her merely as someone she had to "spend time with" because her presence was so draining. This whole time she did not even realize people were purposely trying to get away from her. The whole time she just thought "I don't understand why this keeps happening to me" and blamed others for never having her back. She thought the world was out to get her.

This is a social example of an individual who refuses to really look deeper and understand that problems may stem from the way she sees things and how she deals with others. She has no self-awareness and does not realize that people might be more inclined to be around her if she just changed a few behaviors. "Know yourself" is a key base for every other pillar and is highly connected to your perception of the world and yourself.

It is virtually impossible to exercise leadership if you have not looked inward. If you have not gained the ability to lead yourself. Knowing yourself entails understanding your feelings, thoughts, and the reasons behind your actions. It is about understanding yourself enough to know what your priorities are and the purpose you want to work toward.

This pillar is the first and potentially the hardest to erect on your journey toward leadership. This pillar is the vantage point for three of the ten eyes of leadership that you must open to be successful. The first eye is "self-awareness," the second is "what matters most," and the third is "finding your own personal purpose." Together, these eyes play a pivotal role in how you see yourself in the world around you. That understanding, in turn, affects your ability to lead.

The First Eye: Self-Awareness

If I ask you whether you know yourself well, your answer will most likely be yes; in fact, most people would have a similar answer. Unfortunately, most people go through life without really knowing who they are. Your journey of survival and growth — the quality of your life — depends on the extent that you understand who you are. The deeper this understanding, the higher your chances of survival and growth. We must become aware of the complexity of who we are from our thoughts, our hungers, values, etc. and how they can be the driving force toward our emotions and actions. Self-awareness is key to unveiling all that occurs beneath the surface.

The Second Eye: What Matters Most

Knowing yourself also means knowing what matters most to you. The more we know ourselves, the more we realize the things that matter are sometimes not what we spend much of our lives pursuing. Knowing what matters most will provide you with the right anchors to ground you in what is essential in your life. Such awareness will also guard you against losing your sense of direction or making decisions at the expense of what you value most.

The Third Eye: Purpose

Knowing yourself is the key to survival and growth, because through knowing yourself, you discover your purpose. Your purpose brings (gives) meaning to each and every action you take. By giving you direction and reason, it helps guide each and every decision you take. Exercising leadership is hard without continuously keeping one's purpose in mind.

Have a heart-to-heart with yourself. Mind you, it is no simple task. Knowing yourself sounds easy and speaks to the soul. However, in reality it is difficult. Each and every one of us is riddled with obstacles that prevent us from constructing this pillar. Probably it is one of the hardest tasks you will ever undertake, but working on this pillar can be instrumental. Trust me, it is worth it! It is important to understand that, when constructing each pillar, each eye helps create a foundation for the next to make sure the pillar is as strong as it can be. For example, the first eye of self-awareness is imperative to understanding what matters the most, and then to being aware of your purpose. Each eye feeds and helps open the next. Furthermore, each pillar serves to interact and help others. For example, the first pillar of know yourself is extremely important as a start, for it helps build the rest. How can you interact within a system without first understanding yourself and how your words, actions, and communication styles affect others?

Pillar Two — Know Others

The way in which Emmanuel Macron, the current French president, was elected shows he had a strong understanding of others. Before he was elected, one of his first major undertakings was the "Grande Marche" (Great March), where he sent out people to conduct 25,000 in-depth interviews that lasted about 15 minutes. His target audience was French voters who represented all parts of the country. The information gathered was then used to create his campaign policies and priorities. From this large focus group, he could understand his voters more and therefore win the presidency

On a more personal level, there was a couple that got along well. When they got married after a few years, the wife asked her husband, "So when would you like to have children?" He responded by saying that he did not want any children; in fact, as a young boy he had made this decision. Shocked and sad, both could have avoided this position had they gotten to know each other's expectations before tying the knot. She made an assumption and did not discover a key underpinning for marriage, thus creating discord.

Humans do not live in a vacuum, free from relationships. Failure to understand one another can lead to grave consequences. For instance, many people argue that wars happen due to conflicting interests. Nonetheless, history also shows that nations frequently wage armed conflicts simply due to their inability to understand one another. Because the more we understand ourselves and each other, the more we are likely to create solutions for co-existence and mutual prosperity. As a result, we need to take into consideration the well-being of those around us in order to survive and grow together. To that end, the second pillar is the vantage point for the following eyes of leadership: the fourth eye of "understanding others," the fifth eye of "knowing how others perceive you," and the sixth eye, which makes you aware of "the unsaid." The understanding you get from these eyes will help you adapt yourself to others, bringing people together. In the process of understanding others, you will also gain further insights into the first pillar of understanding yourself.

The Fourth Eye: Understanding Others

Knowing others starts with understanding others. Understanding allows you not only to feel with them, but also to show concern for them. People can sense when someone truly cares about them, and also can tell when understanding is faked to get something from them. Understanding others means truly empathizing with them to the point where their concerns become yours. It is not about abusing that knowledge. Rather, you use that understanding to make a positive impact on the lives of those around you and to build a functional relationship that can support both sides.

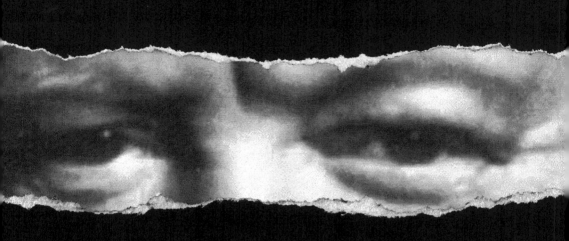

Whose eyes are these?

The Fifth Eye: How Others Perceive You

Knowing others also entails understanding how others may perceive you. Sometimes we think, falsely, that others see us objectively and feel about us the same way we feel about ourselves. It is important to be aware of the signals showing how individuals actually perceive our actions. It is likewise important not to project our own feelings or insecurities onto others. This awareness helps you connect with others and recognize their boundaries, a vital ability when attempting to mobilize others in an act of leadership

The Sixth Eye: The Unsaid

Knowing others means understanding their unspoken cues. People are not always upfront about their intentions. Hence, knowing others is part of being able to see beyond what is actually said.

The pillar of knowing others allows us to build the bridge we need between ourselves and others, because without others, survival and growth are impossible.

Let's take the following scenario as an example: A group of people is stranded on an island and everybody starts panicking. What the group needs is someone who understands the dynamics of each person and the group, as a whole, and knows the best way to calm everybody down to prevent chaos, aggression, and freaking out. Such a leader can inspire them to work in a manner that ensures their survival. Note that it is not necessary for only one person to take on the role of a leader. Any one of them can exercise leadership and inspire their fellow stranded buddies.

With each individual focused on fulfilling the tasks they are best suited for, the whole group can work more cohesively; each piece of the puzzle will be set in the correct place. Leading the group requires us to possess the elements of the second pillar of knowing others, allowing our fourth, fifth, and sixth eyes to "see" with an understanding of the others, of how they perceive us, and what they are leaving unsaid. If we use these eyes effectively along with our other eyes, no one should end up as shark bait!

Pillar Three — Know Systems

Knowing the system is key to survival. I knew someone who was visiting Saudi Arabia about ten years ago, and he was not familiar with the rules and regulations of the system. Therefore, he went jogging in shorts that were quite short next to his hotel. When the police saw him, they arrested him for indecent attire. Had he known the system was very strict about conservative dress, he would not have acted as he did. It is important to be aware of the varying systems that you are a part of; otherwise, one wrong move can get you expelled from the system or sometimes sent for isolation in jail.

Humans have existed within systems since the earliest days of civilization, relying on the systems to survive. By depending on one another, they forged their destiny. Each person would fulfill tasks or obligations necessary for the continuity of the group — the pack or tribe. By sticking together and challenging the forces of nature, humans could reach newer and better horizons. Centuries of working together allowed bigger entities to arise, illustrating that we as individuals can accomplish astonishing feats, but only within systems. Therein lies the importance of understanding systems.

This pillar is especially crucial in today's interdependent world. Globalization and technological advancement have made the world a smaller, yet more complex, place to function. We now rely more than ever on others; on groups, teams, whole organizations, and even vast systems, in order to function, solve problems, and achieve our goals. Just as it is important to know others and the role they play in your life, it is also essential to be aware of the systems of which you are a part, including cultures, countries, or companies. The systems pillar is the vantage point for the seventh eye "systems", which focuses on the unique dynamics of a system; the eighth eye "enemies", which remains aware of any enemies or potential threats to individuals and the system itself; and the ninth eye "the unexpected", which seeks to anticipate unexpected events that can disrupt or threaten the system.

The Seventh Eye: Systems

Each individual must deal with a variety of systems, each with its own distinct set of rules and way of living. Understanding systems includes everyone surrounding you, (e.g. your friends and family). When you go against the system, there are always repercussions. For example, when you are going to your first day of work at a new company, the first things you notice are the practices and culture. What is acceptable? What is not? How will you fit into this web of connections? On your first day, you want to fit in rather than cause a ruckus and have the system turn against you. The last thing you want is to cause the system to not move forward or to feel insecure. We all try to play by the rules in each of our systems or manipulate it to our advantage, so it is important to choose the systems you join wisely — at least, whenever you can choose.

The Eighth Eye: Enemies

When you want to keep a system up and running, it is important to keep watching out for enemies. As important as cohesion is, it is also essential to understand who is not actually on your side. While it is important to the functioning of the system to watch for enemies outside the system, it is also necessary to watch for those who may threaten the system from within.

The Ninth Eye: The Unexpected

The only way to truly succeed as a leader is to be able to deal with any situation and adapt. Even if you have all your other eyes open, sometimes things pop up unexpectedly. And that is when the true test of strength comes.

Understanding systems is key for any leader to truly survive. After they have awareness of themselves and others, the entire system, as a whole, needs to be taken into consideration. Furthermore, it is important that you are aware of your supporters and your opponents, otherwise it will be difficult to survive. Lastly, unexpected shifts will always occur and present a major challenge for a leader: When things do not go as planned, what do you do? How do you handle them? This is the true test of what the leader is made of.

Pillar Four — Know Authority

Knowing authority can be the difference between feeling safe and protected and sleeping on the street! It is often said that people quit their bosses, not their jobs. All of these explanations refer to the intricate relationships that we have with authority. I am sure you can think of hundreds of stories that relate to authority figures at home, at work, in social organizations (churches, charities, book groups), and in the government.

Every system that involves people also involves authority. Authority figures are those who have power over us, by virtue of the position they hold within the group or organization. We all have authority figures in our lives: Our parents, teachers, bosses, or even a policeman. These are key figures who have guided us and affected us in more ways than we know.

Dealing with authority figures will greatly affect your survival and growth, because knowing how to maneuver and work with these figures will help you leap forward in life and in your career — or not. If we constantly have problems with these figures, those problems will prevent us from achieving our potential.

For instance, sometimes authority in a totalitarian state can be too difficult to deal with. One cannot openly speak against such a governing entity in the same way one can in a democracy. Open speech can lead to imprisonment, exile, and even death.

Another example is in business. You cannot work at a company and continuously clash with the owner or your superior. You need to know when confrontation is necessary and when to let things go, because only then will you ensure your professional survival and growth, and the continuous progression of the system. Also, remember that authority has teeth; constantly testing authority will have repercussions like...hmm... let me see...getting FIRED, or even imprisoned!

On the other hand, let's say you are the actual owner of the company. Even you, the almighty big boss, should learn to abide by the legal regulations set by governmental authority figures. Straying away from the law can lead to the government knocking on your door. Would you like to be accused of fraud? Your unfamiliarity with state laws can lead to the permanent shutdown of your organization, or even put you in jail. I don't think any reasonable person would like that, unless they like hanging out with inmates and angry prison guards.

This pillar is the vantage point for the tenth eye, which focuses on authority.

The Tenth Eye: Authority

Understanding authority — how you react to it, how you negotiate with it, and how you assert it — are all crucial to your survival and growth. Authority exists and will always exist in every nation, international organization, and even the smallest neighborhood store. Without authority, it would be difficult to function. Whether a nation has a dictatorship or a democratic government, authority is still present. I cannot stress enough how important it is to understand authority. Wherever you go, you'll find you will always have a higher form of authority exercising greater power than you ever can.

Pillar Five— Know Technology of Leadership

The Rev. Martin Luther King, Jr., was a prime example of someone who had leadership skills without having any formal titles. His ability to communicate his ideas was inspiring and he was one of the biggest names associated with the Civil Rights Movement. He had a profound understanding of himself and others and was able to garner support in significant numbers.

This pillar is about the point when leadership comes into action. One cannot exercise leadership until the first four pillars are erected and their related ten eyes opened and refined. For the fifth pillar to be erected, all the previously mentioned pillars must already be in place. So, before you can exercise leadership in the best capacity, you must understand and constantly monitor yourself, others, systems, and authority.

Leadership, of course, requires a variety of skills, such as communication, negotiation, analytical thinking, conflict management and resolution, etc. These skills are important tools of leadership and helpful in many areas of life. But since they are already covered in many brilliant books and publications, these skills are not the focus of this book. Rather, we are focusing on awareness of the fundamentals of leadership, before going into specific techniques. For the only way specific skills can be used in the first place is by being aware of the fundamentals.

Aside from the specific skill set needed, leadership in our personal lives, organizations, and societies is about utilizing all ten eyes. You cannot understand the technology of leadership without opening up all of your ten eyes. For all the characteristics stated above, such as negotiation and communication skills, all require the awareness brought on by the ten eyes.

As you may have already gathered, I have labeled these ten types of awareness as the Ten Eyes of Leadership because our sight (and insight) is perhaps the most powerful sense we have to perceive the world around us. One cannot expect to thrive and exercise leadership if one is not aware of the information constantly being thrown one's way.

Unfortunately, our physical eyes have limitations and deceive us at times, just think about those optical illusion puzzles. So, these ten eyes are specifically designed to raise our awareness of both what we see physically and what is beyond our physical sight. I have grouped the eyes with the Five Pillars of "The Kouly Model for Survival and Growth" to show how they relate to the exercise of leadership and to make them more accessible and easier to remember.

It is important to keep in mind that anybody can exercise leadership, not just people in positions of authority. Acts of leadership in this book can manifest in the simplest of ways, as long as you are inspiring someone and mobilizing the system to move forward. If you are contributing through mobilization in any shape or form to your own or someone else's survival and growth, then you are exercising leadership. That is how simple it is. However, exercising leadership requires the awareness that comes from developing "The Kouly Model for Survival and Growth" and opening the Ten Eyes of Leadership.

Once you have strengthened the Five Pillars and attained the awareness afforded by the Ten Eyes, you will be able to spot what actions will put systems into motion. You can make more coherent and consistent decisions for the benefit of those around you. The key is to be present and mindful of the information around you and to make enough sense of the world to understand how you can intervene to improve the world.

It is time to open your Ten Eyes and start seeing the world differently — in Ultra HD, perhaps?

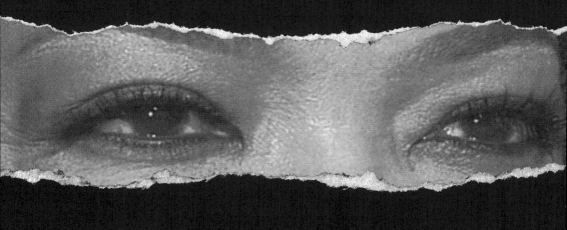

Whose eyes are these?

PILLAR I
KNOW YOURSELF

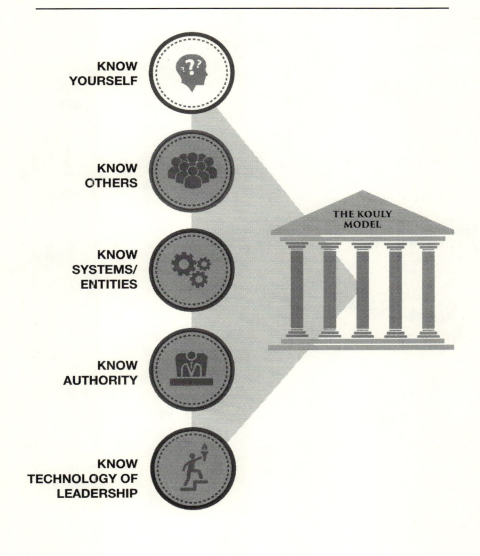

THE TEN EYES OF LEADERSHIP

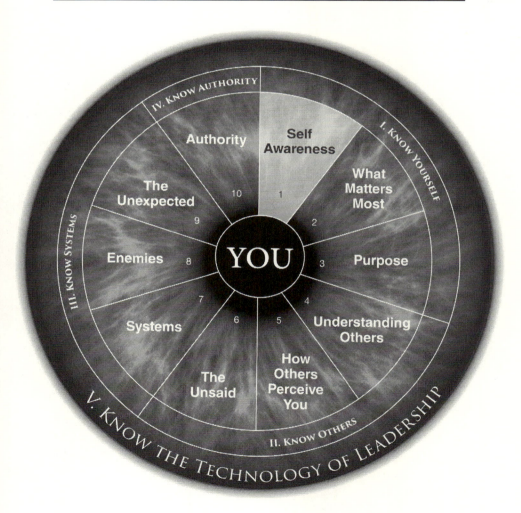

CHAPTER TWO

THE FIRST EYE: SELF-AWARENESS

While our physical eyes are focused on the world around us, the first eye of awareness is an imaginary eye totally dedicated to monitoring ourselves. It is the eye of consciousness and self-awareness that should never sleep.

The first eye can be compared to a security camera recording you from four different angles and giving you data on the following four aspects of your life: What you think, what you feel, what you do, and what you say in any given situation and at any time.

Imagine looking at a monitor with a picture-in-picture option, watching four different movies of YOURSELF on each of the small viewing screens displayed in front of you. Would you be shocked by what you see?

KNOW YOURSELF

THOUGHTS
(What you think)

FEELINGS
(What you feel)

ACTIONS
(How you behave)

WORDS
(What you say)

Screen Number 1: What You Think

Let us take a look at the first screen of the first eye's "security camera." Have you ever taken the time to monitor your thoughts? What were you thinking right before you became sad, happy, or angry? One of the functions of your first eye is making yourself conscious of the power of each and every thought. What if you could record all your thoughts? What story would they tell?

Have You Met Your Brain?

Did you ever try to count how many times you think per day? Or even better, have you ever tried to silence your mental babble and think of absolutely nothing? Let's face it: Even if we want to, we are incapable of rendering our mind a complete blank. Even meditation requires that you focus your mind on something such as your breathing. That's because we do not think. Thinking just happens to us. It is what our brain does, just like the heart pumps blood, the kidneys filter, and the lungs breathe.

Our thoughts, though perhaps not always the most refined, are in fact one of the main reasons for our survival. Our reasoning capabilities are unmatched by any other species on earth.

Brain evolution shows us that the human brain is the largest and most complex of any living primate. It is intricately wired to seek clues, associations, and connections to make sure we do not put ourselves in any kind of danger. Our brains draw us to safety and reward. Such instant and moment-to-moment alertness requires a brain that is working around the clock.

Any form of pain or risk is perceived as danger to our existence and, whether the danger is emotional or physical, the same brain areas are activated. Our brains really do not distinguish between physical and emotional risk. Try to recall a time when you said good morning to your boss and he or she did not greet you back. More often than not, our brains will connect the lack of response to the boss's potential dissatisfaction and start building dramatic scenarios worthy of an Oscar. Suddenly, our job is in jeopardy, our livelihood is at stake, and our entire family is at the risk of starvation and inevitable death!

A less dramatic situation comes to mind: A colleague or neighbor does not reply to your greeting. Although this person does not control your paycheck, and thus does not affect your financial and physical survival, the social rejection triggers a fear that comes from being alone, and this rejection is also perceived as a serious risk. We are social creatures; our brains learned through thousands of years that acceptance and group integration are the keys to our existence. We know that surrounding ourselves with others who will help us get food and stay safe is essential for our survival. Whenever our brains assume we are not liked or accepted by our surrounding social environment, they immediately go into panic mode, showering us with countless thoughts attempting to fix the problem or simply run away from it.

Our brains store all memories of the past, especially painful physical or emotional experiences, within our subconscious mind. However, like a computer, the scope of attention is like the desktop and the subconscious is all the data that is stored on the hard drive. When triggers or warning signs are repeated, it brings forth data from the subconscious — just like when you search on the computer you get data from the entire memory base of the computer. So, although memories are stored in the subconscious, they may, when triggered, be brought back to our scope of attention so that we avoid similar conditions in the future. To keep us out of danger, our brains constantly play "what-if" scenarios of the worst-case situations that could result from our current position.

The brain also uses exaggeration and generalization as mechanisms to keep us safe. If a dog attacked you once, your mind will not take the risk of allowing another dog to attack you. It will simply deduce that all dogs could possibly attack you; hence all dogs are potentially dangerous and should be kept at a distance.

Our minds are rarely, if ever, accurate and objective; the brain amplifies, understates, generalizes, and distorts to avoid any perceived risk. This risk avoidance is why stereotyping and first impressions are powerful. They are your mind's tools to keep you "safe," even though they might be inaccurate.

Note to Self: You Are NOT Your Brain!

Unless we understand how our brains function and why they do what they do, the data we use to make decisions could be misleading. The purpose of the first eye is to keep the brain from automating its assumptions without permission from our awareness. The brain can easily change this assumption when presented with new data. If we monitor our minds closely, we will realize they are totally consumed by keeping us safe and pain-free, both physically and emotionally, and seeking physical and emotional pleasure.

Without the first eye, our brains are destructive, like an elephant running uncontrollably through a busy downtown. The brain will either flee from what it perceives as danger, or it will impulsively go after its desires or whatever attracts its attention. As Jonathan Haidt puts it in his book *The Happiness Hypothesis,* the unconscious mind is like the elephant and the conscious mind is the rider; we must learn how to train the elephant, otherwise it will take us wherever it pleases. The first eye reminds us that we are not our brains; it is our responsibility to filter and re-label the thoughts our minds throw at us. Otherwise, we can become mentally exhausted from believing in the brain's deceptive messages or satisfying all its cravings. And our treasure trove of past experiences can forever color and warp our current judgments.

The first eye acts as interference; a rush of negative thoughts and fearful ideas can take over our brains and rob us of our peace of mind. The first eye gives us perspective, returning us to being present and aware while alerting us to the intruder—the train of negative thoughts attempting to hijack our brain.

Keeping our perspective is not as easy as it may seem. As I write, I can recall many times when I struggled with this very problem. Perhaps my readers who are parents can relate to the following example.

A while ago, I realized that, while on business trips, I would wake up with a rush of negative ideas and concerns about the safety of my daughter and son. My job often required traveling for long periods of time, which meant time spent away from my family. I recall one day in particular when the negative thoughts came over me like a wave; thoughts such as — what if they get hurt? What if something were to happen to them? Other thoughts were more subtle, such as, I am always traveling; am I missing out on important moments of their lives? These thoughts used to keep me up at night, but all this worry didn't solve anything.

Once I became aware of the pattern, I learned how to stop that train before it started up: I reminded myself that certain things are just out of my control, but at the same time, making sure that the time I did spend with my children was memorable and noteworthy.

Training my first eye to be aware of the patterns of thought took a while, and I struggled with it. But the training helped me refocus my thinking and understand why I was thinking negatively and feeling concerned. It is important to understand that feelings are just our reaction to our interpretation of our thoughts and senses. This interpretation can be false, and often it is. By revisiting the origins of the interpretation, it becomes easier to change the story you tell yourself.

Here is the thought process I went through.

1. **What is the nature of my thoughts?** My thoughts are clearly negative ones.
2. **Why is my mind producing such thoughts?** Whenever I notice my brain's chatter, I stop and ask why I am being so negative and fearful, and try to answer this question as objectively as possible. In this example, I believe my mind is trying to help me take care of my loved ones by alerting me to possible dangers they could

face. My mind's reaction could be the result of some bad news I may have heard about someone else's children or parents, or of some movie I watched the night before, or simply physical and emotional exhaustion. In some cases, it may trace back to childhood, when something bad would occur when my father was not around to come to the rescue (e.g. something as simple as a knee scrape). Also, the reaction could be triggered by residual guilt for not being able to spend as much time as I would like with my children.

3. **How accurate are the thoughts that are crossing my mind?** My thoughts are deceptive and not accurate at all because there is no reason to assume that something bad will happen to them.

4. **Is it okay that I continue to think this way?** No, it is not, because the thoughts are making me sad and irritable for no justifiable reason.

5. **Should I allow such thoughts to go through my mind?** Absolutely not. Such thoughts are ruining my day and deflecting my attention from important subjects I should focus on. Perhaps the best option would be to spend as much quality time with my children as possible. That way, I can feel comfortable in knowing I tried my best and some things are just out of my control. Even if I am unable to see them that much, I should think about how the work that I am currently doing is providing for my children and helping them live an abundant life. Thinking through this course of action may help calm the voices.

6. **Are these thoughts really serving me or working against my well-being?** They are working against me.

7. **What would be a better focus of my thinking?** The constructive, useful, or happy thoughts that generate joy or progress would be much better. Perhaps my thoughts could also be a reminder to really be present during the times that I do spend with my children, and to focus on recalling those times when worry starts to creep up.

The same process applies whenever you catch your mind generating any kind of damaging thoughts about your business, future, health, family, loved ones, etc.

Through awareness, your first eye gives you control over your mind so that you regulate the ideas and thoughts it is processing. Instead of being swept away by the flux of data your brain is sending and acting upon, you should filter the data. You then decide whether to either give your brain permission to proceed or ask it to re-label and reframe its interpretation of the situation. Most importantly, your first eye helps you assess the quality, accuracy, and reliability of your brain's messages. Think of your first eye as your mind's watchman; it catches and immediately stops your mind when it is engaging in negative self-talk and maladaptive assumptions or default behaviors that you carry. As in: Do you tend to avoid problems or always assume people have good intentions?

Our first eye also keeps watch over our positive thoughts. Specifically, when our thoughts are unrealistically positive (e.g. overly optimistic, euphoric). It is possible that we will experience thoughts that exaggerate our traits and abilities (e.g. we are smarter than most people, so we can finish this project tomorrow [overly confident]). Although having an inaccurate positive thought may not seem like a bad thing, sometimes having too much of a good thing can be bad. The downside to such thoughts is that we may end up becoming arrogant or self-centered, or we may base our actions on exaggerated thoughts of our capabilities — opening us up to surprised failures and pressures. Your first eye will make sure that such thoughts do not get out of hand, since we are more likely to not give positive thoughts a second look. With self-awareness, you can monitor your thoughts be it negative or positive, constantly gauging the accuracy and reliability of each thought. This will allow you to remain conscious and balanced.

Daniel Kahneman, in his book *Thinking Fast and Slow*, describes the mind as having two systems. System 1 is the unconscious mind — the fast-thinking part of the mind which, for purposes of this discussion, allows negative thoughts to flow through the mind. System 2 is the conscious mind, the slow-thinking, problem-solving part of the mind. In this context, the first eye's duty is to invoke System 2, the conscious mind or slow rational thinking, in order to make the individual realize the System 1 chatter in the mind is not necessarily true. Your first eye allows you to regain control of your mind's focus by putting your attention and energy where you decide.

Remember, the most powerful and frequent voice we hear is our inner voice; this inner voice creates our reality.

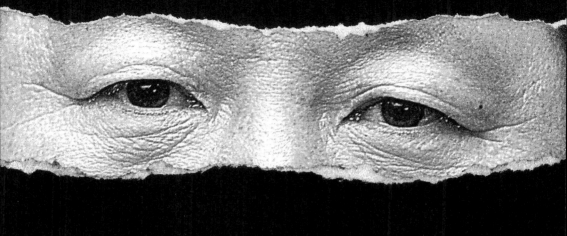

Whose eyes are these?

Helping Your First Eye Gain Control over Your Thoughts

Here are some strategies for using your first eye:

- **Pick a name for your brain.** The next time you find your mind producing negative thoughts, let your first eye send it a mental note saying: "Sami, enough!" or "Stop the drama, Sara!"

- **The power of refocusing.** Our minds cannot process many things at the same time; consciously diverting the mind's attention to something more positive will keep it from indulging in dramas. Do not waste time trying to fight or suppress your thoughts. The more you focus on an idea, the more your brain uses the neuro-connections related to the idea and the more ingrained the idea becomes. Instead, use the awareness resulting from your first eye to replace your mind's chatter with more affirmative thoughts. Bring back a happy memory, think of something you are grateful for, repeat a mantra, say a prayer that comforts you, meditate, or do whatever it takes to gain some clarity of mind.

- **Be present.** While your brain is oscillating between your past and your future, let your first eye bring it back to the present. Whenever you find your mind wandering, focus on your breathing, on the sounds, images, colors, and scents around you. Try to engage your mind in picking up signals from your surroundings instead of remaining stuck on its internal rollercoaster.

- **Keep your body busy.** The moment your first eye unveils a mind drama, tune into what your body is doing, instead of allowing it to rerun distant memories or magnify worries about the future. Exercise. Go for a walk. Swim a few laps. Sing. Dance. Volunteer.

- **Write it down.** Sometimes putting your mind's conversation on paper is all it takes to expose the childish basis of the thoughts. If nothing else, writing down the conversation gives you a better understanding of what is going on in your head.

- **Think of other interpretations.** When you feel defensive about someone's behavior, instead of taking things personally and immediately jumping to negative conclusions, take the time to think of other interpretations of the current situation. Sometimes our first reaction is to imagine the worst-case scenario and act accordingly, but assuming the worst will only contribute to excessive defensiveness.

Practice

Instead of surrendering to our brain's drama, we must learn to stop and question what is happening:

- What is the nature of the thoughts that are going through my mind?
- Why is my mind producing these kinds of thoughts?
- How accurate and objective are the thoughts that are crossing my mind?

- Is it okay that I continue to think like that? Are these thoughts really serving me or working against my well-being?

- Should I allow such thoughts to go through my mind?

- What would be a better focus of my thinking?

It takes awareness and presence to notice that you are getting sucked into a whirlpool of negative thoughts. But with practice, you will slowly begin to notice that you may feel as if you were hearing your first eye shouting, "Hey! Stop! Enough."

How We Make Decisions

Listen closely: your decisions — the ones you make on a daily basis — are rarely your own. Are you shocked? It's true. This is also a key to understanding other people.

Each person is made up of voices; voices from each person they interact with, from the dominant individuals such as the mother or father, to the fleeting friends and acquaintances. We are layers of voices made up of experiences that we have gone through.

Whenever we undertake a decision, we consult these voices, resulting in an unconscious tug of war. For example, if you are in college taking an exam, and by accident you overhear another student say the answer to a question you were unsure of, and you look down at your paper and realize you have the opposite answer — then the voices begin. Your mother tells you it is not right to cheat; keep the answer you had originally written. Your teacher's voice tells you this exam is to demonstrate your knowledge; overhearing another student is not your knowledge. Then your hungers, or false needs, start to edge in, saying, you really need to do well on this exam; you can't afford another failure and this question is worth a lot of points. What do you do? Which voice trumps the rest?

This is a small illustration of the tug of war occurring every time you make a decision. The key is to be aware of these voices and actively decide which one to listen to. The first eye is important in this situation for the following reasons.

There are many times where we will make decisions unconsciously because we feel that they are the "right" thing to do. But in truth, it is just because we have been conditioned to think that way. Only with awareness of the voices can you start to make your own fresh decisions.

Let's take another example, you are choosing the career path you want to take. This, for most, is a fairly large decision and ultimately a turning point in your life. So, what happens? The voices start an uprising. Your father wants you to take over the family business; your mother wants you to be a lawyer; your own hungers tell you that you want something that will help you reach international acclaim. In the end, however, the only way to decide on your own is to be aware of the voices and, at the same time, to silence the voices. It is important to silence all these voices in order to hear the one voice that is most important to making your decisions — your own. To really, truly discover what you want. Is it to be the lawyer? To take over the family business? Or to follow a completely different path? Once you silence the voices, the decision will be in your hands.

Screen Number 2: What You Feel

The first eye's "security camera" shows your feelings on its second screen.

Being Aware of What You Feel Matters

Consciousness of an emotional state and the ability to manage it in various circumstances sets certain individuals apart from others. The widely held assumption that IQ is the only criteria for success was challenged over the past few decades when research showed that people with normal IQs overtook those with the highest IQs seventy percent of the time. It became clear that raw intelligence as we knew it was not the sole predictor of personal and professional accomplishment.

This first eye's emotional awareness is not only important in families and social relationships, but also in the working world. As a matter of fact, the higher your position in an organization and the larger the organization, the more vital the role of the first eye, because the impact of any inappropriate emotional response increases with the level of responsibility. The response is sensed throughout the whole organization. Think of it this way: A motorist's blind spots are dangerous, but not as lethal as those of a school bus driver. Emotional awareness is key, and the more you are responsible for, the more important it is.

How often do you wake up feeling that a black cloud hovers over you, and you can't shake this feeling all day? When you feel down, and somebody asks you why, do you have an answer? Perhaps you respond with, "I really don't know. I guess I woke up on the wrong side of the bed."

For many, this scenario is far too common. Before you are really aware of your first eye, the feeling could last for hours and you would not know where it came from. It goes without saying that these feelings have a cost, and sometimes a heavy one. The first casualty is, of course, you. The more you allow your feelings to linger, failing to identify their nature and source, the more you lose precious moments of your life that you could have enjoyed.

The second casualty can be people around you. As much as you want to believe that your feelings are well-hidden and only affect you, it becomes clear that your feelings are in fact visible to all. What you try to hide with silence comes out through other channels. Body language, tone of voice — these all change, sometimes without you realizing it.

One example comes to mind. One day, I came back home from a very stressful day at work, drained before even entering the house. As I entered my room to change into something more comfortable, I became annoyed because I could not find the comfy clothes I was looking for because my closet was rearranged. Already irritated from work, I made an angry comment about the arrangement of my closet. My wife was pregnant at the time and already in an emotional state, and the comment hurt her feelings making her cry. As this happened, my then 6-year old daughter, Maria-Helena, walked into the room and said very assertively, "Daddy, mommy is crying, and the baby inside her is crying, and now I am crying…Tonight is the worst night of my life. Was it really worth it?" Her statement resonates with me, till this day. It was one of the most powerful lessons that I received, and it was from my 6-year old daughter. So, before you allow your disruptive feelings to best you, remember: Is it really worth it? and at what cost?

Unfortunately, the problem was not just with my angry comment; as emotions are contagious. The negative energy that I had received from work had to go somewhere, and it was transferred to my wife and eventually my daughter and even my yet unborn son. I never realized how much of an effect I had on others until I had managed to ruin not only my night, but everyone's. Had my first eye been awake, my awareness would have prevented my reaction.

Negative energy does not stop once you have let it out; instead, you have just lit a fuse that keeps moving on. Never underestimate the impact that your mood can have on others! The first-eye awareness helps you deal with your feelings in a more constructive manner.

This Phenomenon Has an Evolutionary Explanation

Our emotions and feelings are there for a reason, even when they make us feel highly uncomfortable. We are biologically wired to be hypersensitive to signals of danger; this sensitivity kept us alive in threatening environments. When faced with a wild predator, it is better to be shaken by a terror so intense we run for our lives, than to sit calmly and rationalize about the approaching menace.

For example, when a herd of deer is drinking water from a lake and one of the animals senses a possible threat, the instinctive reaction is to run away from the danger with a warning sound to the other deer. The other animals don't wait to investigate the reasons behind the signal and judge their validity; instead, they immediately mimic the first animal's state of alertness.

We humans do the same thing. Feelings are contagious because they are signals coming from the environment around us. When another person shows signs of seeing some danger, our instinct mimics the feeling and we become equally alert. This instinctive reaction happens because we are more sensitive to detecting and reacting to life-threatening danger than we are to safe and secure states in our environment. Negative emotions are more quickly spread than positive ones.

Emotions Are Neither Good Nor Bad They Just Are

We are a bundle of emotions; we are all carrying around stories of pain, guilt, shame, anger, and sadness, as well as tales of love, connection, happiness, pleasure, and pride. Yes, even your callous boss or your thick-skinned ex whose insensitivity is chilling.

Each of us experiences a wide spectrum of feelings, but only a few of us accurately recognize them as they arise, much less expresses them in a healthy manner. Emotions are the expression of our feelings. They are neither good nor bad. They just are. They are energy manifested in our body as a response to thoughts and external stimuli — and there is nothing we can do to avoid them. It is the way we handle this energy, and the following reaction, that is dysfunctional or harmful, not the emotion itself.

For example, you feel jealousy and sadness when you discover that the man/woman of your dreams is actually married. This sadness and jealousy is painful, and your natural reaction is to get rid of the feeling. You see the feeling as a threat, so your brain tries to fix the situation right away. If your brain can't fix things, you turn to distractions such as Mr. Alcohol, or other forms of drugs such as Netflix and a bowl of popcorn. Few people will actually be aware of the emotion, own it, and understand that eventually it will pass. But awareness is the starting point. Instead of trying to push out the feeling and get rid of it, try to take away the power it has over you. Admit the feeling to yourself; sit with that feeling while understanding it is just that, a feeling. Meanwhile, try to stay out of trouble while waiting for it to pass, and avoid allowing it to color an unrelated judgment (your self-worth) or action (your eating habits).

Consider the positive side of some apparently negative emotions. Fear is a natural warning designed to shield us from danger; it is neither a negative emotional response nor a weakness. Anger motivates us to protect our boundaries and our loved ones. Sadness is a natural expression of the pain that results from a loss we experienced. These emotions are often seen negatively, but the only time they become destructive is in extremes. Emotions are indispensable, having a great impact on the way we live our lives, relate to others, and lead our businesses and communities.

Decoding Our Emotional State

We must learn to identify and accept our feelings and emotions as natural and normal expressions of our humanity, without allowing them to hijack our lives. The first eye is an energy detector, helping you pay attention to how energy manifests itself in your body. The first eye sends a signal when you might be overly tense or unrealistically hopeful. It is a calm internal voice providing hints that you have become defensive or irritated. The first eye encourages you to be honest with yourself and recognize the nature of your feelings and their potential impact on you, your relationships, and your performance at work.

The first eye sheds light on the feelings we experience, helps us notice any change in our mood, and traces the meaning of our feelings. The first eye asks, and answers, questions such as: Why am I feeling tense? Why did my heart clench at the sight of this person? Could my jaw grinding be an indication of stress or anger that I am trying to hide? Why am I breathing so heavily? Do those "butterflies" in my stomach indicate love?

For example, I had a friend who had a problem with jealousy/bitterness. But he did not even recognize that he was a jealous/bitter individual. Whenever his colleagues or friends succeeded and received praise and attention, he would belittle their achievement just so he could feel better about himself. Had his first eye been activated, he would have realized his jealousy was the root cause, and he would have recognized his negative undertones when supposedly 'praising' his friends for their achievements.

In another instance, a friend of mine told me about the time he decided to stop donating to charity. It seems that at first he was giving money out of the goodness of his heart, but when people began to praise him for his generosity, he chose to temporarily pause his contributions. The reason, he said, was that he discovered that his initial motivation to donate changed from pure charity to enjoying the praise that he was getting for his generosity. His first eye helped him understand what the real reasons behind his positive feelings were— the attention and praise he received. He knew that these feelings caused him to forget why he was donating in the first place and he therefore decided to stop. It is important that we not allow our positive feelings to become maladaptive, at times seeking that "good feeling" at the expense of others' well-being or at the expense of our compassion and empathy.

On a more personal level, when I was a war journalist I was exposed to many tragedies. It had become common to lose friends, colleagues and acquaintances. After some time, I became desensitized and numb to death and loss. I would attend funerals and feel nothing, despite my sometimes close relationships with the deceased. Using my first eye I was able to notice my apathy, understand the reasons behind it, and work on restoring my emotional sensitivity to its original state.

Since our feelings are triggered by our thoughts, answering the following questions will make you more aware of your feelings:

- **What is the nature of my feelings?** Am I feeling fear, anger, jealousy, excitement, peace, joy, pleasure, or something else? Do I have predictable triggers for these emotions (hence, buttons others can see and push)?

- **Why am I feeling this way?** What does this data tell me?

- **What thoughts are encouraging these feelings?** What triggered these feelings and why do I react to the triggers this way?

- **Are my feelings justified?** Am I overreacting? Could there be another explanation that I have discounted?

- **How are these feelings impacting others?** Are others around noticing? Are they affected negatively or positively?

- **What do I do with these feelings?** Should I indulge them or let them go, by changing my thoughts and perspective?

The above questions apply to each case individually; the answers will change as your feelings change. Understanding your feelings starts with awareness. Once you identify your feelings and isolate the thoughts or situations that triggered them, they will become easier to manage so that your words, actions, and ultimately your life aren't controlled by your unbridled feelings.

Our Feelings Can Be Altered by Changing the Way We Think About the Situation

In order to change the way we feel about a situation, we must first change the way we think about it. Our thoughts generate feelings that in turn are expressed in emotions. Luckily, we are capable of controlling our thoughts through conscious awareness. We can become the masters of our own minds.

Our first eye allows us to understand, direct, and possibly modify our emotions. We may still experience negative moods and compulsions, but with awareness we do not act upon them on a whim. We wait until the urge passes. Our subsequent response will then be from a place of awareness and purpose; it won't be just an instinctive reaction to feelings.

Deeper Than the Tip of the Iceberg

We often struggle when attempting to express our current emotional state in words, limiting our replies to a plain "I'm feeling bad," or a flavorless "I'm OK."

The first eye invites us to look deeper into our emotions, beyond the tip of the iceberg. Once we start reflecting on the nature of our feelings, we can pinpoint whether "bad" actually means "irritated," "frustrated," "demoralized," "anxious," "ashamed" or "depressed." The more precise our description is, the better our understanding of how and why we feel as we do, and what we should do about it.

Every emotion we experience carries data about ourselves. Awareness is about learning to listen to the data instead of getting carried away blindly by emotions.

As Carl Jung said, "Everything that irritates us about others can lead us to an understanding of ourselves." Developing the first eye requires us to ask, "Why is this person or situation irritating me or generating this emotion? To what extent does my feeling reveal my personal issues?"

Every time we overreact, the first eye helps us stop and reflect. It helps us see how the issue built up over time. The emotion is an indication that we have ignored our emotional clues, and are now reacting out of our inner turmoil. Similarly, the first eye notifies us when we are attempting to suppress our emotions and keep them locked inside. The first eye is the awareness that resonates within us, reminding us that emotions are energy in motion, meant to flow freely. Blocking their expression is not healthy.

Our Biology Tells All

Did you know the chemical composition of our tears varies depending on the reason behind the cry? Researchers have shown that, unlike reflex tears naturally generated to keep our eyes moist or protect them following an irritation, our emotional tears contain toxins and hormones affecting our mood. Studies reveal that letting these elements out of our bodies through crying helps balance our stress levels and creates a sense of relief.

The Key to Performance and Thriving Relationships

Failing to find a healthy way to express our feelings and keep our emotions in check can challenge our survival and growth. As Sigmund Freud puts it, "Unexpressed emotions will never die. They are buried alive and will come forth later in uglier ways." Unexpressed feelings tend to fester and will inevitably affect those around us, one way or another. Moreover, unidentified emotions are often misunderstood by others, as well as ourselves, leading to irrational decisions and damaging behaviors.

How can you expect to develop healthy personal, business or social relationships without being in tune with your emotions? We all want to be around people with whom we get along, people who remain composed under pressure, who are pleasant, and who inspire trust and predictability. We want to surround ourselves with those who do not get upset easily and can keep their feelings in check. It is difficult to deal with individuals who allow rage or resentment to create mountains out of molehills.

Exercising Leadership Requires All the Data You Can Use. Blind Spots Can Kill You

The awareness of our emotions is undeniably a key factor in creating and sustaining healthy personal relationships. Emotional awareness is an essential foundation to our survival and growth, helping us exercise leadership.

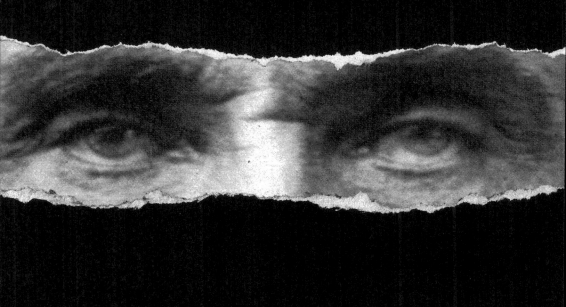

Whose eyes are these?

Screen Number 3: The Way You Behave

On the third screen that the first eye's "security camera" shows us, we can see our own behavior — if we are willing to watch!

The Real Cost of Chewing Gum

During a Strategic Leadership class that was videotaped and given to top executives, something happened that will always resonate in my mind. Sitting in the first row was the CEO of a famous technology company: An elegant woman in her late thirties with a strong presence whenever she entered the room. However, she had one habit that detracted from her presence and proved to be a nuisance to everyone around her. She had an obsession with chewing gum, and whenever she was chewing, it was loud. Really loud. Snap, Crackle and Pop had nothing on this woman!

That was the first thought that came to my mind when I saw her looking at the camera and boldly chewing her piece of gum at eight in the morning. We had just started the session, and it became clear that her presence in the video would be highlighted by special sound effects. Let's just say it was a highly audiovisual morning!

You would be surprised by the noises coming out of such a seemingly graceful individual. Even more surprisingly, she was totally oblivious to her behavior and sat there, fully engaged in the conversation, popping bubbles and chewing with her mouth wide open.

Regardless of how lovely she looked prior to the gum spectacle, she had now lost her status in the group as her snapping and popping eroded her charm.

The video session lasted one hour, and afterward the session was replayed on a large screen. Literally seconds after the replay started the lady jumped off her seat and switched the projector off.

"This is not me," she choked. "No…no, no, this is not me," she repeated, totally embarrassed by what she saw.

"I am sorry, but this is you," I said with a smile. "We have all watched you live for an hour. Now it is your turn to watch yourself and see what we have seen. This is my gift of awareness to you."

Though she pleaded not to have the video played, we ended up watching the entire session. She occupied the largest part of the screen, as she was the closest to the camera.

"Is this how I usually look?" she bashfully asked her second-in-command, the senior vice president of the company.

"Yes," he answered. "Can I be more honest?"

"Please do," she said, trying to conceal her uneasiness by covering her face with her hands.

"You are like this in the office, at meetings with clients and during social events. Actually, I have rarely seen you without a piece of gum," he calmly shared.

"Oh my God…I have chewing gum in my purse, in my office

drawers and in my car..." she said, blushing.

After the painful realization of how her conduct appeared to others, she never chewed gum again. You can imagine, however, the unintended impressions she had already made and the many opportunities she had previously missed by failing to see how something as simple as chewing gum could so horribly ruin her image.

The same applies to every one of us. Whether we are at a corporate meeting or out on a date, we certainly do not want to make a bad impression. We are biologically wired to try our best to always be looking good, being right and feeling happy; we are designed to survive and grow in peace and joy. Yet we often find ourselves stuck on autopilot, unintentionally acting in ways that hinder our well-being and best interest.

Take a Hard Look at Yourself

Everything you do either adds value (to your power, to your reputation, to your position), or takes it away. Whether or not you acknowledge the impact of your behavior, everyone around you feels it and will interact with you accordingly.

The bottom line is that your behavior will dictate what happens to you. This is a fact of life. You reap what you sow. **As a result, you have three options:**

1. You can choose to stay in the dark, ignoring your behavior, and die this way — snapping, crackling and popping. You may occasionally wonder why life doesn't make sense, or why people react to you in specific and odd ways, but you soon drift back to oblivion.

2. You can be lucky enough to have life slap you across the face with the hard truth (in the form of, perhaps, your vice-president, wife, daughter, boss, or a total stranger). This might work, but it will hurt. You should hope that it wakes you up before it is too late.

3. You can choose to be more conscious of your behavior by simply opening your first eye.

Your first eye will help you become aware of how you present yourself to the world. It will make you reflect on the impact of your interactions on both yourself and others. It will reveal perspectives on yourself that you previously failed to see.

If you think of it, there are only two types of interactions, with a positive and negative version of each. You make your point either by saying or by doing, or by not saying or not doing. There are no other ways. Words have an impact, but actions speak far louder. Your behavior is a strong manifestation of your thinking; it reveals who you are. It is like making a statement in **bold**. <u>Underlined</u>. And highlighted in yellow. Each and every one of your actions carries a meaning. Whenever you do something, you send a signal — about yourself, then about your intentions, thoughts, and feelings toward others.

The questions raised using the first eye are:

- How is the way I am acting or not acting contributing to my survival and growth?

- Is what I am doing (or conversely not doing) adding to or subtracting from my standing and image?

- How should I behave in order to live a meaningful and dignified life?
- How will what I am doing affect my position within the system?
- Will my actions help me move forward? or cause me to remain stuck?

The first question is, in fact, the fundamental question, relevant to all the screens of the first eye's security camera. You may notice that these questions are related to the five pillars. To answer the first question, to know whether your actions contribute to your own survival and growth, you must know yourself, the first pillar. Your standing and image is what others know about you, which is the reflection of the second pillar (know others). Asking whether your actions move you forward or leave you stuck addresses the third pillar of knowing the system you are in and understanding the effect of your actions on the system. Knowing your position in the system shows that you know authority, the fourth pillar. And finally, answering these questions will show you the way to the fifth pillar of leadership skills.

> Be aware of your behavior and make sure that it serves your survival and growth.

Practice Makes Perfect, But Pay Attention to What You Practice

We are creatures of habit, and by nature we do not like major changes. When we fail to keep a damaging behavior in check, however, it gradually becomes rooted in our routine.

It is said that if we do the same thing for three weeks, it becomes entrenched as a habit. Whether or not that specific time frame is a myth, behavioral patterns do form after constant repetition. By giving us the gift of self-consciousness, the first eye prevents a dysfunctional behavior from hardening into a habit. The first eye alerts us when the same action is replicated in different situations, such as binging on chocolate whenever we are nervous, adopting a sloppy posture, or leaving the room whenever a conflict arises. After all, if an action once led you astray or caused you trouble, why would you let it develop into a default behavior?

Once we are aware of the dysfunctional behavior, it becomes our responsibility to make sure that the outcome of our repeated behavior is meaningful and serves our well-being and that of others.

You Are Now Entering an Area of Personal Accountability

Can you think of a friend who has been in and out of at least five relationships within a single year, who claims to have been cursed with the most horrible boyfriends/girlfriends? Can you think of other friends who seem to be stuck in the same cycle of problems at work, business, career, or family? At what point would your friends acknowledge that this "serial bad luck" might actually be more than just luck, that your friends might personally be part of the problem?

When something in our life is not working, the first eye invites us to take a long, hard look at our behavior and ask, "What am I doing that is contributing to or sustaining the situation that I am complaining about?"

Instead of passively complaining, we need to approach our problems in a more responsible way. The first-eye awareness can bring about a change in our life by shedding light on our own responsibility. Awareness frees us from the illusion of being victims of life's circumstances or people's cruelty; awareness gives us the power to shape our lives.

The Butterfly Effect

Besides affecting our own survival and growth, our actions also impact others, sometimes significantly. Not only does our behavior portray to the world a certain image of ourselves, but through our behavior, we also reveal to others our thoughts and feelings toward them.

You cannot propose to your girlfriend whom you have been with for four years, and then feel uneasy when she starts suggesting wedding dates. You cannot dance the night away with Liz, your junior trainee, at a corporate event, then lash out at her the next morning, saying, "Ms. Smith, your report is long overdue. I expect a more professional attitude from you!"

Make sure your actions send the right message

Be careful — every action you take impacts those around you, and you cannot act without people noticing. Every action has a meaning, and consequently causes a ripple effect. Trust me — you cannot stop the ripple once it begins.

Every behavior will evoke a chain reaction, firing up a series of other reactions, making your life a set of dominos falling around you. So, before you act (or fail to act), be sure to set up the domino pieces so that the final result or picture turns out to be meaningful.

You Break It, You Buy It

Life rarely offers you a get-out-of-jail-free card. If only! Instead, you will be held accountable and responsible for your actions.

When you miss a red light and kill someone, you cannot tell the judge, "I apologize. I definitely did not mean to kill him. I was in a rush...it was kind of urgent."

When you sit in an executive meeting the same way you sit while tanning on the beach, don't be surprised when that promotion, you had been eagerly waiting for, "no longer exists," or that your attempt to lead an initiative within the organization is not being taken seriously. Your actions come with a price. You have to decide whether you can afford that price. Impressions matter. You must be fully aware of your actions and their impacts. Are your actions leaving the right impressions? Are they knocking over the right dominos?

Regardless of the situation or the goodness of your intentions, the system will reward or punish you according to your behavior, especially when you are exercising leadership and are under the spotlight. Most of the time, it will make you pay for your behavior with interest and a few extra taxes you did not even know existed!

It goes without saying that keeping your first eye open is more demanding in harsh times than when things are going smoothly and on cruise control. This is not convenient for those who buckle under pressure, who panic, freak out, or freeze. But it is important to continue doing what you need to do regardless of the pressure; make sure that you are acting in the manner you feel best serves your survival and growth and that of the people you are trying to lead.

Don't Leave Your Helmet On

He was around 30 years old. At least, that's what was written on his resume, and quite an impressive one it was. There was just one tiny hiccup during the interview — I did not see his face. He spent the entire twenty minutes answering my questions with his motorcycle helmet still on. I am not making this up. The worst part is that he had no idea, not a single clue. So how do you tell a bright, intelligent (wish I knew what he looked like) man that the reason he did not get the job was because I prefer seeing the face of the person who is applying for a job? Just imagine his reaction when he realized: wait a minute, my head feels a bit heavy...

Everyone knows how stress can make people freeze or not be fully present in the moment. What saddened me the most was that the candidate had all the right credentials. He obviously did not mean to keep his helmet on; he was merely nervous. That day, my boss from my early career days said something that has resonated with me ever since, "Your intentions are irrelevant. What matters is what you do." At the end of the day people cannot see your intentions; they can only see your actions.

You may be the smartest person alive and have a pristine and faultless resume; but, if you are not conducting yourself properly, not being fully aware and present, then a resume is just words on paper. That is why the first eye is crucial, because it brings you back to what is important, shakes you up and says, "You may want to remove the huge clunky helmet off your head; it could be slightly distracting."

> *Every Breath You Take. Every Move You Make.*
> *Every Smile You Fake. I'll Be Watching You.*

That is the first eye's promise to you.

The first eye notifies you every time it senses mixed signals from your side. It raises a red flag whenever what you say is incompatible with what you do; whenever your actions do not serve you well.

The first eye invites us to ask before every leadership intervention we start to make, whether we are really sure of what we want (as opposed to acting out of compulsions or false "needs"), and whether what we are doing will actually get us there. If necessary, the first eye calls for a corrective intervention. Gradually, our behavior will become functional and purposeful.

This active awareness is similar to what the Jesuits call "contemplation in action." It is about being in tune with your body and senses. It is about being inside the action and at the same time outside; acting on stage and simultaneously watching your performance from the theater's balcony. Active awareness is realizing as you give your speech that you have been looking at the same corner of the room for some time and ignoring the rest of the audience. It is about noticing, while telling your team you are open for suggestions, that you are defensively crossing your arms. It is about being aware of that chewing gum popping in your mouth, or that helmet on your head.

I, Robot

In no case should the first eye limit our spontaneity. Good awareness should never happen at the expense of our authenticity and instincts. The purpose is not to become rigidly self-conscious of our behavior to the point where we become robots.

The trick is to be sure you are aware of the consequences of your actions and feel that they serve who you are.

The need for the first eye boils down to this: How much does your radar REALLY catch? How much are you, the scientist, altering the outcome of the experiment?

With Great Titles Comes Greater Responsibility

As much as behavior is important for our personal survival and growth, and as much as behavior impacts our relationships with others, there is a far greater effect from our behavior when we hold power or are authority figures. Anyone with the responsibility for a family, team, department or even a whole organization knows the effect of rash behavior on the rest of the group. Corrupt behavior at the top is far more contagious than pompous motivational speeches. People imitate what you do far more than they listen to what you say.

Exercising leadership and mobilizing others toward a clear set purpose requires having what it takes to be in the spotlight. If you are a pilot flying a 747 jumbo jet, you'd better realize the effect your actions have. If you panic, so will everybody else. When the spotlight is on you, everything you do is amplified. So before taking any action, carefully consider the impact your interaction will have on your system.

Screen Number 4: The Way You Talk

This final screen shown by the first eye's "security camera" includes an audio track to show how you talk.

Imagine having to listen to a speech like this: "Time and time again I have been admired for my many accomplishments in the field of psychology, as well as in the field of speech communications, and my work with children with disabilities. But it got me thinking, with all these degrees and experience, why have I not learned more? The field of research is so extensive that years of experience only allowed me to merely scratch the surface of what is and could be in the field of psychology. I am humbled by the work of the scientists before me because they have taught me a great deal about perseverance, sticking to a goal, and striving for excellence, even when it seems hard, even when it may be impossible, even when people say that you cannot do it, even if at times you feel you cannot do it. But, sadly, after all this motivation, I realized that I did not do their words justice. I did not live up to the name that I had so very much admired."

We are all familiar with this type of digression; phrases get stacked on top of one another and both the speaker and listener lose track of the original idea. The first eye brings awareness to the way you talk to others, monitoring the content of your speech and the choice of words. It listens to your tone, assesses the speed and frequency of your interactions, checks your facial expressions, and most importantly, appraises the context of the conversation. The first eye hints at whether you are rushing your presentation or whether you are so slow that someone in the back row is dozing off. It invites you to use pauses and silences, but only to your advantage, not lasting so long as to be awkward. It indicates whether your voice is shaky or confident.

Self-awareness of your speech asks questions such as:

- Do I carefully listen to others during a conversation? Or do I tend to do most of the talking?

- Am I being vulgar? Am I being loud? Am I being clear?

- Am I talking too much? Too little? Too fast? Too slow?

- Am I being too silent? Why am I not acknowledging my right to take part in this conversation and say what I have in mind?

- Are the words I am using appropriate to the cultural context? Do they accurately describe the reality I am referring to?

- Am I being coherent or rambling aimlessly? Is my speech focused?

The Power of Words

Of all the creatures on this planet, we are the only species to develop language in order to connect with the external world. Our words are not merely sounds that simply convey information; they are much more elaborate than that.

Words have power. What we say and how we say it can advance or destroy our relationships, careers and the well-being of our community.

Our Words Tell a Story

We are often unaware of the power that language has on our lives. At first glance, language seems to be merely a communication tool we use to connect with others. In reality, language is the mind's operating system; our spoken words are the direct expression of our thoughts. A glance at our speech can reveal a lot about us. As a matter of fact, our speech exposes our beliefs and values, which can be empowering (I am smart, I am capable) or limiting (I will never be good enough).

You can learn a great deal about what's going on in your head simply by paying attention to what you say. Your words carry to the outside world the movie that your mind is playing, or at least a small preview of it.

A Sneak Peek of Your Future

Here is an exercise to show how your speech may be affecting your future.

1. Complete the following statement: "I am..."
2. Take a few minutes to write down as many more answers to that statement as you desire.
3. Now read the list out loud.
4. Notice the effect on your feelings, your expression and your posture.

What you say about yourself is not simply a reflection of who you are; it creates who you are as an individual. What you say about yourself affects your confidence and shapes your subconscious . Your body believes what you say. It is really a vicious cycle: What we say is a reflection of who we are, but who we are is affected by what we say.

The more we use the same words, the more grounded our belief becomes. Gradually, the language that we use becomes our internal bylaw.

> *"Words not only affect us temporarily — they change us."*
>
> -DAVID RIESMAN

The role of our first eye in what we say about ourselves is to question whether the belief we are holding onto is serving our survival and growth.

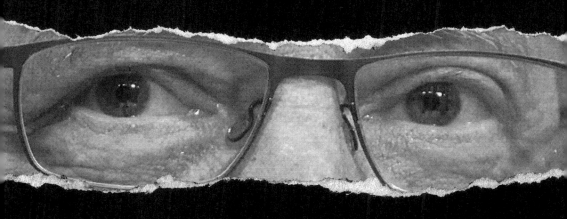

Whose eyes are these?

In our executive leadership programs, one exercise helps participants identify their worldviews and beliefs by anonymously completing a list of words with the first adjective that comes to mind. For example: "Life is… " "Marriage is…" "Failure is…." You would be surprised how much you can learn about a person from his or her choice of words.

Is What You Say Really What You Want to Say?

Think of an emotional state that you have been through this week, and choose the word that best describes it. Think of a problem you have been facing at work or in your relationships and try to illustrate it using words of your choice.

You will be shocked by how inaccurate your choice of words can be, especially in tense situations. We can easily distort the truth by using incomplete statements, generalizations, and many other patterns that hinder our communication and misrepresent our reality. The first eye invites us to take an objective look at what we are saying and to confirm whether we really mean it or not.

- "His behavior is **killing me**" (Is it really killing you or is it merely an annoyance?)
- "The presentation was a **nightmare**."
- "I'm **dead**."
- "I'm **broken**."
- "My boss **never** listens to me."

- "It will take me **forever** to finish this assignment."

Using accurate words matters, because words have such a powerful impact on our minds that any lack of accuracy in our spoken version of reality twists our view of reality. Without awareness, we start basing our future behavior, emotions, and thoughts on what we believe and talk about, instead of acting upon what is true.

> **Our words define our reality. The more accurate and precise the words we use, the better we define our experience.**

Where Is Your Focus?

Our attention is directed and focused through language.

When our speech is weak and scattered, its impact on others will be diluted. Human attention span is limited; even advertisers have only about fifteen seconds to catch us. That's why advertisements go wild and crazy to grab our attention. That's why every few seconds, cameras change angles in a movie scene. To retain the attention of our audience (including ourselves), we must have coherent, easy-to-follow speech.

The quality of our speech also reflects the quality of our thoughts. An old French saying states that what is clearly thought of is clearly communicated *(ce qui se penseclairement, s'enonceclairement)*.

In addition, when our words focus more on restrictions than on possibilities, the words blind our ability to see the situation with fresh eyes and find a solution. In fact, many words we use carry a sense of limitation within them; words such as "I can't," "I won't," "It's impossible," etc. Also, some words that don't even have a negative connotation can limit or deny us our freedom, such as "I should," "I must," "I have to," etc.

After much practice in awareness, whenever our speech becomes directed toward identifying faults rather than highlighting opportunities, our first eye will hint that our speech is starting to impinge on our growth. The first eye keeps us constantly aware that, through our language, not only are we creating our own self-identity and experience of life, but we are also shaping that of our families and teams.

When used on a regular basis, limiting words will curb our control over the situation, restrict our creativity and set us up for failure by conditioning us to feel helpless. Without even realizing the impact of our words on our lives, we become unconsciously programmed to fail.

The first eye, when opened, indicates when our choice of words is inappropriate and limiting. It urges us to use words that will contribute to our survival and growth. For instance, instead of saying that you "can't deliver the project," you consciously ask for the help and resources (time, training, money, etc.) necessary to make it happen. Whenever your first eye catches you assuming that "I could never run the meeting like he does," or "I'm not good at delivering speeches in public," it invites you to reframe your statement in a way that does not generate a future you wouldn't want to be in. In fact, since the past tense focuses on blame, and the future tense focuses on solutions, often we can improve our futures just by reframing past-tense statements ("I've never been good at speaking") into future-tense statements ("I could learn a lot about speaking.") The last thing you want to do is stand in the way of yourself by limiting your potential.

Ask yourself the following:

- How often do I think about my choice of words and their impact on my life?

- How often do I use self-limiting words?

Impact of Words on Others

The impact of our words goes beyond shaping our inner self and defining our reality. Words have the power to evoke change in the world around us.

Every sound wave is an energy flow that we are spreading around. Through our words, we constantly communicate to those around us whether we are a threat or an asset to their survival and growth, and whether we have enough power to help or harm them. Our words reveal not only our intentions toward others, but also our power and ability to make a difference in their lives.

- Do your words hold hints of danger or threats?

- Do they imply dominance or arrogance?

- Do they portray helplessness or weakness?

- Does your speech project influence and resourcefulness?

- Do people take you seriously?

Picture a young boy, whose personality is like fresh dough ready to be molded by those around him. Now imagine this boy's future if all he hears as a child is, "You will never make it in life," "I wish I never had you," "Stop being a baby — boys don't cry," and "You are worthless."

Now compare that scene to a father telling his children, "If you ever catch me saying 'I can't,' I will give each of you a dollar bill."

> "But if thought corrupts language, language
> can also corrupt thought."
>
> - GEORGE ORWELL

Words have a fascinating impact on our emotions. Our happiness is regulated by words we say and hear. While a single word can uplift us, another can easily ruin our day. It is not only our choice of words that matters, but our timing. Even praise, if it is untimely, can be a source of confusion and tension, whereas a well-timed reprimand may restore a sense of peace. Thus, the first eye helps us become conscious of every aspect of our words and their impact on those around us, keeping us from blindly identifying with our thoughts and feelings of the moment. Regardless of our emotional state, our first eye helps us consciously weigh our words and decide whether they serve a purpose.

Link to Leadership

Our communication plays a big role in how we exercise leadership, because the impact of words multiplies when they are spoken by a leader. The larger the group you mobilize, the broader the impact of what you say. Leadership requires clear intervention in a situation, and that clarity in turn requires a deliberate choice of words with an appropriate delivery. The last thing you want when addressing your system is to use weak words, or to undermine your position and credibility through your speech.

The first eye's role in speaking is to alert you when you are not capturing the audience's attention, which could happen because you are excessively apologetic, you look away as you speak, your tone of voice is monotonous, or your choice of words reduces their impact. The system will not take you seriously if you shyly introduce your opinion. Similarly, the system will not be inspired if you cushion what you are going to say with an excuse of why it is probably wrong. Perhaps you find yourself hiding behind sentences like, "I'm sure you know better but..." or "This will probably sound absurd..."

Mobilizing others is about using words that inspire people, not words of discouragement and hurtful criticism. Your family, department, organization, and community need your ideas. However, unless you learn to share them purposefully, without arrogance or apology, yet with clarity and focus, you will miss chances to make yourself heard and make a difference in the world around you.

The first eye is the calm awareness reminding us to use our words purposefully. The first eye encourages us to speak with compassion and humility, keeping in mind the humanity of the person on the receiving end.

When used properly, our words have the power to change the world.

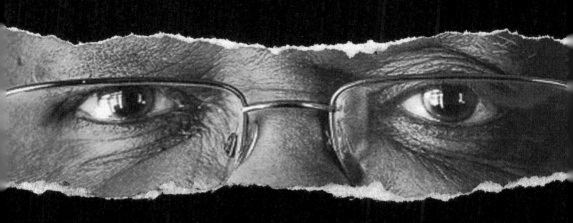

Whose eyes are these?

THE TEN EYES OF LEADERSHIP

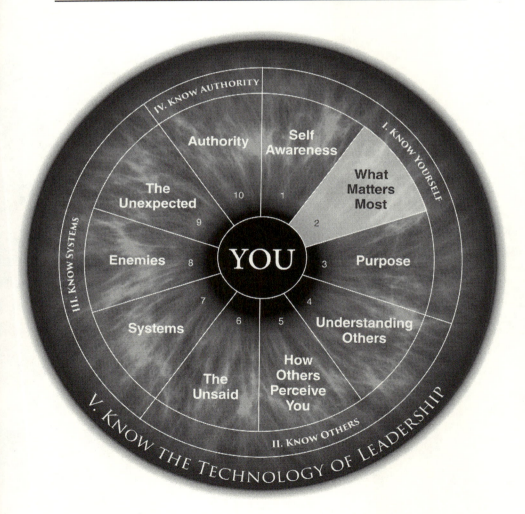

CHAPTER THREE

THE SECOND EYE: WHAT MATTERS MOST

Imagine that today is your last day on earth. I know the thought may be disturbing but please go with it; it's important. It is your last day on earth and you only have about two minutes to send a message to the most important people in your life. Who would those people be? What would you tell them?

In moments of panic, when we are pushed to the breaking point, we tend to remember the things that truly matter. It is not the expensive car, house, or clothes you buy. It is not the job where you spent tireless hours trying to make it to the top, thinking the top position means you are something. Family matters to us, and I don't mean only your biological family, but your chosen family as well. What matters is the people who mean the most to you in the whole world; the experiences you shared with them are the ones you really care about. In the end, you are not going to remember that beautiful watch you bought; you are going to remember the first time your child smiled at you. You will remember the first date you had with that special someone. You are going to remember your parents' love. It may sound cheesy, but if you were to take your last breath today, whom would you want to talk to or see? Those people are most important to you.

The second eye is there to remind you, each and every day, what really matters. When you must decide between working overtime and catching your son's sixteenth birthday celebration, or when you must decide whether you have time to visit your sick friend in the hospital, refer to your second eye, and it will guide you. Life is about choices, and it is important for us to keep our priorities set correctly. So, what really matters to you?

Make sure that what matters the most is first on your list of priorities.

Keep Your (Second) Eye on the Prize

"How different our lives are when we really know what is deeply important to us, and keeping that picture in mind, we manage ourselves each day to be and to do what really matters most."

- STEPHEN R. COVEY

Did you ever make a big deal out of something, only to regret how you made others feel as a result? What about that time your spouse begged you to go out, but instead you just wanted to play video games? Or the time your grandmother really wanted to see you, but you made up some phony excuse about work?

What you devote most of your time to reveals what you truly care about. I doubt you have ever heard someone say right before passing away, "I've got to fix those accounting sheets I left on my desk." Or, "I did not make my deadline. My boss is going to be so angry." So why do we give more of our time, attention, and patience to work, to silly addictive games, or to social media, rather than spending quality time with the people closest to us?

This does not mean that the most important thing for everyone is family and loved ones. For some, their careers, seeing the world, or devoting themselves to giving back to the community are their priorities. If that's what makes you happy, then those things should be placed at the forefront. The second eye is about digging deep down inside and figuring out what really matters at your core, then letting that understanding guide each and every one of your decisions.

Many people do not realize what is important until they are staring death in the face. Bronnie Ware, a nurse in palliative care, noticed over time how people became more aware in their last moments of life. It was as if suddenly what used to seem important was no longer so important. People change and prosper immensely when faced with their own mortality. She observed five particular regrets she heard over and over from patients:

1. "I wish I'd had the courage to live a life true to myself, not the life others expected of me. "

2. "I wish I didn't work so hard."

3. "I wish I'd had the courage to express my feelings."

4. "I wish I had stayed in touch with my friends."

5. "I wish I had let myself be happier."

Sometimes we get so stuck in old habits and patterns that we forget what truly matters. Do not let that happen to you; remember that time is fleeting. We think we have plenty of time, but the truth is we do not. Re-connect and place the important things first in your life, or in the end, what truly matters will slip through your fingers.

> **Keeping your second eye on the prize means letting what matters lead the way.**

That's What the Schedule Says

> *"The key is not to prioritize what's on your schedule, but to schedule your priorities."*
>
> - STEPHEN R. COVEY

Have you ever had one of those to-do lists that runs on for miles? Although you would like to think sometimes that you could do it all, there will be times, even if they are rare, when the list will get too long. The list will be the kryptonite to your superpowers; the arrow to your Achilles' heel. Sometimes you just need to ask for help or delegate. Sometimes you simply need to say, "No."

Prioritizing is about trade-offs; you must recognize that, if THIS gets done, then THAT won't. Afterwards decide which task is vital. Knowing what matters helps you make those decisions quickly and easily.

> *"You have to decide what your highest priorities are and have the courage — pleasantly, smilingly, non-apologetically — to say 'no' to other things. And the way you do that is by having a bigger 'yes' burning inside."*
>
> - STEPHEN R. COVEY

Choose Your Friends Carefully

Which friends do you feel you can be completely yourself with? Life is too short for chitchat and gossip or spending time with someone who secretly wants you to fail. Spend time instead with those who bring out your best sides, not the vengeful, conniving, and superficial sides. Be with the people who put a smile on your face, who love you for yourself, and do not try to change you.

Invest in the relationships that actually matter, not the ones going nowhere. Invest in relationships that lift you up, not drag you down. The friend, partner, or family member who does not put forth any effort, or make any attempt to meet you halfway, is not worthy of your time and attention. Any relationship involves a form of give and take. It is up to you to find the right balance and not get sucked into relationships that continuously drain you. It is time to either place the necessary boundaries and stand up to these people, talking through what is bothering you, or to cut them loose. Either way, nobody deserves to be dragged down.

Your friends or the people with whom you choose to surround yourself are the people you will come to resemble. We are social creatures, greatly influenced by those around us. So, choose people you respect and look up to. Choose someone from whom you would not mind learning a thing or two.

Ask yourself:

- Do these people bring out the best in me?
- Are they encouraging me to be more resilient and to pursue opportunities of growth?
- Can I depend on their support when I need it?
- Do we have conflicting values?

> You become like the people you spend the most time with, so choose them carefully.

Make Your Time Count

> *"Now and then it's good to pause in our pursuit of happiness and just be happy."*
>
> - GUILLAUME APOLLINAIRE

We get so caught up sometimes in thinking that, if I just buy this house, I will be happy. If I just find someone to be in a relationship with, I will be happy. If I just get that promotion, I will be happy. If I ace this test, I will be happy. There will always be something more to venture on to, another goal to attain. But sometimes, and this is quite important, we need to stop all this planning and hoping and just enjoy the moment.

Enjoy what you currently have instead of dreaming of how it could be better. If you have a loving family, spend time with them and enjoy their presence; not everyone has what you have. If you have a job you love, stop thinking about promotions and enjoy each day you get paid to do what you love; many people do not have that. If you have a spouse, take the time to express your love and appreciation for him or her; not everyone has that.

Life is not about what you could have; enjoyment involves appreciating the here and now. Most people procrastinate, believing they have more time than they do. When you live like there is no other day than today, you start to appreciate what you have right now. But appreciating today does not mean refusing to plan ahead or dream. Enjoyment highlights the importance of appreciating the process of getting there, and of recognizing what you currently have.

"Time flies whether you're wasting it or not."

- CRYSTAL WOOD

The Goals of Tomorrow May Not Be the Goals of Today

Childhood. A time when you thought everything was possible. What about the girl who thought the best profession in the world was to be a doctor? So, she always used to wear a plastic stethoscope and pretend her dolls were sick. Only later did she realize how the sight of blood nauseated her and how harsh are the life-and-death situations doctors face.

As you grow older and face reality, sometimes the dream you used to envision, that mattered so much, begins to look different. Things that seemed so important back then become almost trivial and silly over time. So, do not be surprised or saddened by the change in what matters to you. In fact, as we mature, there must always be some readjustment and adaptation. Your dreams will change, and so will your goals. However, never allow these changes to discourage you from dreaming and setting goals; it is goals and dreams that keep us moving forward.

We are not static beings; change is inevitable.

What Directs You?

"Every morning we are born again. What we do today is what matters the most."

- GAUTAMA BUDDHA

The second eye requires purpose. It is vital that you know why you do what you do. If you focus on day-to-day tasks instead of the bigger picture, your happiness will probably also be short-term.

Here are a few questions to spark your curiosity and shed awareness on your purpose (that will be delved into further in the third eye):

- If you were to look back at your life right now, what would you celebrate as most important?
- What memories matter the most?
- What parts of your life motivate you most; what do you wish to excel in?
- If you continue in your current lifestyle, what will your life look like in ten years? Twenty years?
- What excites you? What makes you feel alive?
- What can you let slide? What activities can you stop doing without a major negative impact on your life?
- If you had one year left to live, how would you spend it? With whom?

These are all important questions intended to make you aware of what truly matters in your life. Once you have discovered what truly matters, your second eye keeps you always aware of what matters most.

Some people may be discouraged, feeling their goals are "impossible," that there is "no use." Of course, some goals are impossible; most of us will never be the fastest man alive. But often a truly impossible goal can be modified to suit our own uniqueness (be the fastest in my age group in a local marathon), creating an achievable goal. Besides, most of the time, we don't set impossible goals for ourselves, just goals that feel impossible (losing fifty pounds, for instance). We need to recognize that, while the goal is possible, achievement may take longer than we would like.

When you have a goal in mind, don't expect it to result in something right away; what is important is that you keep making incremental progress. Just break it down and take it one step at a time. This makes the goal more plausible and less daunting. It is also essential to stay on top of your progress, making the steps a priority and accomplishing each step as soon as possible. Of course, completing the steps may interfere with other aspects of your life. At that point, you make the hard choices, the sacrifices or compromises for what you deem important. You need to decide what your goal is and what is essential to accomplishing it, and prioritize things today in view of your future goal. It may help to imagine looking back on the present from the future, asking your present self what you did today to become that future self.

If my goal is to become a proficient piano player because playing the piano brings me joy, and I absolutely love it and have since I was a child, then I need to practice, and practice hard. I will not accomplish my goal if I allow other activities to get in the way of my practice time.

Sometimes it isn't a matter of knowing your priority, but trying to find the time for it. We get caught up in trying not to disappoint others and sometimes lose out on what we really want. It is important that your top priority gets the necessary attention, so do whatever it takes.

What matters most to you can range from your family and friends, to your faith, to your true passion (your purpose), to the love of your country, or even your love for animals. It is up to you to decide what matters the most.

Find what matters most and be patient enough to take the needed steps toward it.

What Matters for Leading Others

In order to exercise leadership, we must be at peace with ourselves. If you are still not placing what matters most as your top priority, how can you lead others toward what matters? For instance, if not being able to spend time with your loved ones makes you feel stressed out, preoccupied, and worried, how can you excel at work?

The first pillar — knowing yourself — forms one of the most important pillars of leadership, but how can you know yourself if you do not know what matters to you? When individuals understand themselves, they can make quicker and better decisions, a vital ability for leadership, survival, and growth.

The concept of what matters most also applies to the business world. For example, in an organization, knowing what matters is fundamental. If you are trying to lead a team without your "eyes on the prize," you will get caught up in mundane and irrelevant tasks. Your time and your efforts will be wasted, and your project will veer off track.

Know what you want, to know how to lead.

No Room for Regrets

The importance of the second eye is its differentiation between what matters and what does not. Once you are aware of the difference, you have mastered an understanding of yourself that some people never achieve.

But the learning curve is steep. It takes time. You won't suddenly become an expert in using the awareness of the second eye just by reading about it. The truth is the hustle and bustle of life can get the best of us. Try to take some time, perhaps five minutes a day, to reflect on what truly matters. Are you spending enough time with the people you want to spend time with? Are you working toward your dreams or stuck in a job you absolutely hate? But remember the words you speak to yourself as you do this. If an answer is 'no,' reassess and make corrections in a positive, future-oriented manner.

We all move at our own pace; there is no one size that fits all. There is also no use in living in the past, wishing you had done certain things or spent more time with certain people. Many people live in their regrets, and see the future as bleak and meaningless. But you have a choice; if you want to be aware and lead your life, you can. You have a choice to wallow in the past, or begin building your future.

The time is now. You can let go of what could have or should have happened and work toward what you want to happen. If you are not going to start today, then when?

Whose eyes are these?

THE TEN EYES OF LEADERSHIP

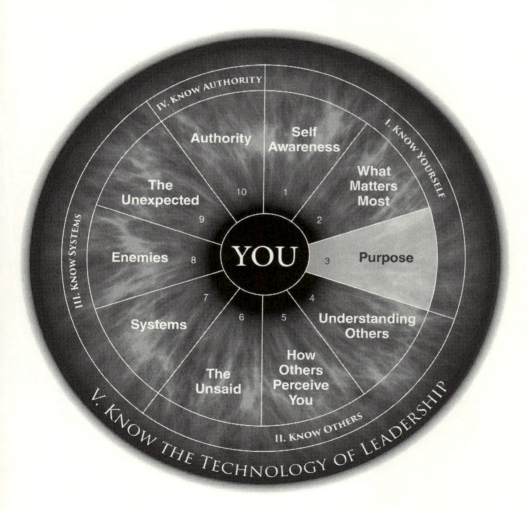

CHAPTER FOUR

THE THIRD EYE: PURPOSE

"Don't ask what the world needs. Ask what makes you come alive and go do it. Because what the world needs are people who have come alive."

- H. THURMAN

Dashrath Manjhi was born in 1934 to a poor family in Gahlour village near Gaya in northeastern India. He spent his life working in the fields; for him, that was the only life that he really knew. Every day, in order to reach the fields that he worked in; he was forced to cross a very dangerous path, and a long one. One day as his wife was crossing the path to bring him his lunch, she fell and injured herself badly enough that she did not survive the wounds. Devastated by her death, Dashrath picked up some tools and started to burrow through the hill. It became his way of dealing with his grief. For years, he slowly chipped away at this hill until he made a passageway that was much safer than the previous one, all by himself. People at first thought he was crazy, but eventually his sheer perseverance and commitment made him something of a legend. Today, cars are able to pass through the passageway he created; he accomplished all of this with just a hammer and a purpose. The grief he felt helped him begin his journey to becoming the 'mountain man,' but eventually purpose kept him going.

What Makes YOU a Diamond in the Rough?

Dashrath Manjhi did not have any special talents. He was not born to privilege. However, one experience changed the entire course of his life. Uniqueness can come in many different ways: From the experiences you have undergone, to your inherited characteristics, such as your mother's smile or your dad's humor, to your mind and the way you see the world. It also can take form in the talents you worked tirelessly to hone and perfect.

Many individuals may have a passion for art, but not everyone with a passion for art grew up in an unstable home, or also loved to act. The idea is that we can all share certain preferences or talents, but it is a unique blend of all our experiences, natural talents, acquired talents, and preferences that make up our unique qualities. Did you know that there is someone out there with a passion to take care of the elderly? He enjoys it so much that he would be willing to do it for free. Additionally, who would have thought that a love for rodents could translate into saving hundreds of lives? Bart Weetjens was capable of training rats to detect landmines and eventually to detect tuberculosis in individuals. Uniqueness comes in many shapes and sizes. But it is up to us to be aware of our uniqueness.

At the end of the day, each and every human being is unique. You will never be repeated. From now until the end of time, there will never be anyone like you. We all have unique talents, interests, and quirks, all of which can hint at what brings our purpose to life. I am not attempting to be inspiring; I am merely stating the facts. Did you know that there are no two snowflakes exactly the same? Likewise, no two humans are ever exactly the same.

Our uniqueness means that each and every one of us will have a different contribution, because we each see things through a unique lens.

Therefore, it is important to tap into these differences and find a way to use them to create value. That is when purpose enters the mix.

What is Your WHY?

Your purpose is your WHY. Why we do what we do; why something exists. Once you have established an inventory of what makes you unique, purpose results from taking this list and really deciding what you are passionate about and what can add value. For example, if you like animals, biology, and you are good with finances and business, you can decide to become a veterinarian and open your own clinic, or you can adopt sick animals and take care of them, etc… It sometimes is not that clear, but you get the idea.

Purpose normally does not have to be just one thing. There are numerous purposes in your life. For instance, in your relationship with your spouse or partner it maybe: ensuring a fulfilling relationship between the two of you. Another example is your purpose as a parent: making sure your children grow to become healthy, functional, adaptive and successful human beings.

But the purpose we are discussing in this section is your core personal purpose, one that can give your journey great meaning, something that brings you to life. Every individual and every organization has a purpose, and it is important to know what that purpose is and to always keep your purpose guiding your way.

Although your purpose can be part of what matters to you most, your purpose is much more specific to your individual journey of growth. If you take care of other elements of what matters most (such as your family and friends) but forget about your own purpose, you will not be entirely fulfilled. Your purpose uses your unique qualities (your experiences, your inborn talents, and your acquired talents) to contribute to the survival and growth of yourself and others.

Purpose is the intersection point between what makes you unique and what you truly love to do, which adds value to those around you. It is about living your authentic self and sharing it with others.

There are many different philosophical ways of looking at purpose. But what it boils down to is the following. The laws of nature, in general, will always support things that contribute to the survival and growth of all. The more you are able to give, the more you will reap the benefits. For example, the more trees you plant the more crops and food you will have. But if you are unwilling to take the time to build the foundation and plant the tree, you will be left hungry. Based on John Nash's *Equilibrium Theory,* the best for the group comes when everyone in the group does what's best for himself and the group. Purpose has a functional value in doing just that. Purpose is about finding what you love and what makes you unique, something that you enjoy, then sharing it with others and contributing to the benefit of all.

If we look at it purely on a survival level, anything that is useless, that does not contribute, eventually dies out. Nature does not spend energy on something that does not contribute to the functioning of the eco-system, as a whole. Eventually, everything that is not able to adapt and provide use slowly dissipates. It was proven that certain biological differences in animals that contributed more to survival eventually became more present in the species. For example, the giraffes with longer necks were able to reach more food and hence were more likely to survive and procreate. Therefore, over the years the neck of the giraffe slowly became longer.

For humans, however, it gets a little bit more complicated. Humans do not function just for survival, they need growth as well. Furthermore, given our social nature our survival is optimized in groups. So, purpose combines our need for growth with our contribution to the group's survival. The reason that we are each unique is because we can each contribute in different ways, which can help us grow and add value. Unfortunately, with humans, purpose is not always as clear-cut as with animals. For example, bees are needed in order to pollinate flowers, and from the second they are born, they know what they need to do instinctively. For humans, our purpose usually comes in the form of something we love to do, what makes our heart sing, something that we would do for free (although it's never that easy to figure out). The key is that, once you learn you love it, you must devote the needed time and effort to perfect it as your craft. For some, purpose can even be about allowing them to find meaning. The main point is that purpose is about finding a way to show your true colors and contribute, which ultimately helps you and the group.

For example, a friend of mine has always loved working with his hands. His face showed sheer joy whenever he was building something new. Would it make sense for a man like that to work behind a desk? Your passion, what makes you come alive, is the key to your true purpose, and your third eye should always make you aware of that purpose. I could tell you about another person, a history buff, who loves travelling the world and viewing historical sites. She has dressed up as important figures from periods throughout history, and re-enacted some of the most memorable moments of history. This individual's experiences and interests all led her down a single path. She became a history professor and an activist who works to preserve and restore historical sites. Her purpose was to make sure we did not forget our history — the events that brought us to where we stand today.

Find out what makes you come alive and let your third eye steer you toward it.

Not All that Glitters is Purpose

To truly grasp what purpose is, you first must understand what it is not.

Purpose is not about your hungers.

Psychological hungers are needs that an individual requires in order to feel balanced and fulfilled. Hungers include: A need for contact/connection and physical touch, recognition, and attention, or a need for novelty and excitement. Hungers are very personal and are related solely to the self. However, purpose is not about fulfilling these hungers. It is about something greater than yourself. It is a need that you are filling within society. It is about bringing out your unique self and using your strengths to move yourself and others forward. It is not about giving in to your craving for hungers such as acquiring money and fame.

For example, I knew a man who postponed his marriage so he could make enough money to buy a Porsche. It is safe to say his wife-to-be was not so thrilled about the matter and left him. This was all based on his deep-seated hunger to be seen. Another example: A well-to-do business man who had millions of dollars but still felt he wanted more. In an attempt to feed his hunger for power and attention, he ran for public office, not because he wanted to make a difference or truly loved it. However, the position consumed him; at least the seeking attention part, to the point where he neglected his business. After some time, he no longer had a spot in politics and returned to find a failing business. He eventually lost all his money and to this day remains in debt. Hungers can blind you to your purpose, for hungers focus on the self, while purpose focuses on service and contribution, and building something outside of the self. In a way, purpose helps you find yourself by giving you meaning along with everything you do.

Purpose is not competition

It is not about being the best or trying to be the best. Purpose is about being the best version of yourself. When you compete, you place a limit or a benchmark on how you should be. Whereas, when you just aim for becoming a better version of yourself, limitations melt away. When you focus too much on the other competitors, you forget to take your own unique path. Similarly, organizations that just focus on competition only try to improve upon what already is out there; they do not try to think outside the box and create something unique and different. What do I mean by this? If you have a talent for creating electronics, you will not just seek to duplicate what already exists. What would be the point in that? No, the point would be to create something different, something that does not already exist. Hence, there would be no competition for your product, which will be on a level of its own.

Purpose is not excellence

Purpose is not about perfecting your craft. That can be an element of your uniqueness, but that is not what purpose is about. Excellence refers to refining your skills, while purpose is focused on what you will do with the skills once refined. It is not about reaching perfect standards, but about living your true and authentic self.

Purpose is not about 'relative' visions or dreams

A vision ends once you have achieved it, and so does a dream. But purpose is more likely to be defined as a concept that you need to embody; purpose does not have an end date. It is ongoing and there are many methods and routes to achieve it.

Purpose is not about blind passion and motivation

Unguided passion can be a very dangerous and volatile thing. Individuals such as Hitler had blind passion and motivation and others got caught up in the bloody mayhem. In another case, individuals such as hobbyists or collectors sometimes spend their money pursuing their passion at the expense of their own or their family's financial security. For example, I knew someone whose passion was to collect art sculptures. Although this seems like a positive, harmless passion it had negative consequences. He would dip in to his family savings to buy these sculptures, at times placing his family in a financial crisis. In addition, he only allowed a select few to view his collection, as such his passion did not add value to others in his society.

Purpose entails not merely feeling passion but directing it toward the betterment of people around you and society as a whole. It must add true value to others and not cause harm.

Purpose is not short-lived enthusiasm

Purpose is an ongoing process, as stated before. It never really ends, and it becomes a way of life. A way of living your true authentic self. Therefore, it is not something that you should pursue for a short while and then quit midway. It needs to become a way of life.

Purpose is not winning

There is no such thing as winning or losing when it comes to purpose. Winning assumes that someone has to lose in order for you to win. Purpose is about contributing to all; so, when you fulfill your purpose, everyone 'wins' to some degree. There is an African word 'Ubuntu' which means 'I am because we are.' This describes beautifully how the world is interconnected. Everything you do affects others; hence the focus should not be on winning, but uplifting yourself and others. This would mean that purpose is not about beating others, or being first, or trying to be the best. It is merely about bringing out the best parts of yourself to contribute to survival and growth of all.

Purpose is not ambition

Ambition can sometimes blind you and limit the journey to just getting to a certain destination. For example, members of a company may defame others to steal the other person's position. Blind ambition can drive you to do things not in line with your ethics, because you are so engrossed with achieving something like power, money, or influence. Ambition may be disguised as a psychological hunger to fulfill some unmet emotional need. However, it can be a strong asset when focused on purpose. Ambition needs direction, which derives from purpose, but on its own may sometimes be volatile.

Purpose is not about money

Money is something we all need, since we cannot all devote our lives to causes and never get paid. But the idea behind purpose is the following: To do something that you truly love, that makes you come alive, provides a benefit to society, and ultimately provides you with meaning. Nonetheless, if there is a financial or business element to the service that you are providing to the best of your ability by serving passionately and authentically (serving with purpose), then it will ensure the loyalty of customers and the flow of money. For example, if you are an aspiring politician and you truly make a difference in your position, you benefit a lot of people because it comes from a place of authenticity. There is no doubt that people will notice this and respond in kind, by voting for you again.

If your purpose is to sing, and you sing for no other reason than your pure love for the art form, then people will notice and be drawn by your passion. When someone cooks a meal from a place of love, versus a place of obligation, you can tell the difference. That is what purpose is; you can spot those who are doing something because they love it, rather than because they must do it, or who have ulterior motives such as money or fame. But once again, if you are providing a service with authenticity, then customers will feel it and reward you through money. But that should not be the focus; the focus should be purpose.

Purpose is not about YOU

As mentioned earlier, we are social creatures, and our ultimate purpose is to survive and grow. But this can only happen by helping others in order to help ourselves. If you just focus on your needs and forget the other, eventually it will come back to haunt you. For whether we want to believe it or not, the world is very much interconnected. So, purpose ranges beyond you; it must if it is to push society forward. How much would the world have missed if individuals like Oprah Winfrey chose to keep talent to themselves? Furthermore, the benefit goes two ways. Every time Oprah did her show and revealed her uniqueness while enjoying it, so did the audience.

Purpose is not about setting records

Purpose has nothing to do with proving to yourself that you can climb the highest mountain, or swim the English Channel. Purpose is deeper than that. If you do end up accomplishing such feats, your purpose may entail motivating others to push themselves beyond their limit and never give up. But the act of breaking a record is never the purpose, just part of a larger purpose that involves contribution. Sometimes people set records or want to be the best in order to fulfill their own hungers, and deal with their own insecurities, but purpose reaches beyond that.

Purpose is not extraordinary

You do not have to become a legend to follow your purpose. Sometimes purpose can resemble a teacher who motivates her students to unleash their potential. Purpose can look like the photographer who captures beauty with the click of a camera. Purpose can resemble the doctor who saves lives daily, or the custodian who makes sure people have clean places to sit. Anything you do can resemble purpose, as long as it adds value to those around you. Each individual making their contribution no matter how small, in the service of others, must be considered extraordinary. You do not have to be the next Michael Jackson or Michael Jordan to find your purpose; it is about being your authentic self.

Purpose is not romantic

Purpose is not a romantic concept, fantasy, or an idealistic notion. In fact, humans in general crave meaning. Meaning gives people drive and motivates them to move forward. Purpose gives you just that — the drive to make something of yourself, to tap into your beauty and special nature. Viktor Frankl, an Austrian neurologist and psychiatrist, in a discussion on his experience in concentration camps, said individuals who had meaning, who had something to look forward to, were most likely to survive. Therefore, purpose is not a romantic concept, but a necessity for survival.

Whose eyes are these?

Searching for a Treasure: Finding Your Purpose

"Let yourself be silently drawn by the strange pull of what you really love. It will not lead you astray."

- RUMI

Much of the stress in our lives comes from living a life that misaligned with our true nature. Stress comes from us trying to be something that we are not, or mask something that we are. Living your authentic self not only is good for you, but for everyone around you. It will almost feel like you are free to be and act in a way that really represents who you are.

When you are living an authentic life, feelings such as happiness will naturally play a larger part in your life. But to get to this stage is not easy. In fact, it takes a long time and many times we fall back to the comfort zone bounded by our fears and insecurities. To be totally authentic takes a lot of courage, but purpose provides that for an individual.

You must remember that purpose is not limited to a specific role. For example, the purpose of an architect is not to be an architect. Their purpose could be to create beauty or design creative and innovative homes. If they stop working as an architect, this does not mean they no longer have this purpose; they can teach others to create beauty or find other ways of creating meaning.

Obstacles on the Road

There are many obstacles that can stand in the way of someone who wants to fulfill their purpose. One could be our need to conform and be like others. Straying away from the norm can sometimes be scary, but if that is what you truly love and want to do, then you must embrace your uniqueness and take that leap. It could also mean getting rid of the need for approval from others. When you find your own unique path, there will always be skeptics along the road. It is important to keep moving forward anyway.

At times, the only thing that really stands in the way of living your authentic self is you. Although you know exactly want you want and who you are, a part of you still does not accept it. You are afraid of how you may fit in, or whether you will gain approval, so you do not even accept these parts in yourself. Lastly, as I stated before, it needs a lot of courage. Purpose does not come easy. I wish it did. It takes courage to step out of your comfort zone and show the world who you truly are.

An individual will not be able to see their purpose if they do not change their perception first. We as individuals sometimes get held up or trapped in our own negative beliefs about ourselves. For example, many people live in order to satisfy their hungers, so they will live a life chasing superficial things that are not meaningful, only to realize that they are never really satisfied.

Other people will become so enveloped in their own wounds and pain that they will never have time to look beyond their own concerns to help or contribute to those around them.

For example, an individual who just went through something difficult (like a divorce, loss of career) in their life who cannot get past their own pain even if a significant amount of time has passed.

There are a few who will not believe in their own significance, and dismiss any notion that they are special or have a specific purpose to fulfill. This happens when we silence our hearts and focus mainly on the fears we have. Fears such as: Not succeeding, not being seen, or not being loved. We then become consumed by these fears and see only them, instead of looking toward our potential and what we could become.

It takes time and a lot of awareness to come to terms with these obstacles, to realize when you are consumed with your own thoughts, or are providing excuses, not from logic, but from fear, or fear of the unknown. Removing these obstacles is a crucial step, but takes time. Be patient with yourself.

What Makes You Shine?

Once you have figured out the obstacles potentially standing in your way to discovering your purpose, the next step is to really discover what makes you shine.

Ask yourself the following questions:

- What makes me shine?
- What makes me so happy that I could do it right now for free?
- What did I love doing as a child?
- What hidden talent or interest have I always been curi-

ous about unlocking?

- If I had no limitations, what would I choose to do?
- What would I do if all my insecurities were quieted?
- When do I get special praise?
- With the strengths that I have, what is the biggest contribution I could make to those around me?
- Who inspires me most?
- Who would I like to be like?

Each of these questions tackles a very important aspect of purpose. Your purpose is never something that you dread; in fact, it brings out the best parts of you, the happiest parts. But purpose is not a selfish endeavor; it is sharing the best parts of you with others.

Once you have discovered your uniqueness, you must ask yourself: How can I use this uniqueness to benefit others? What problem can I solve? What opportunity can I create? This questioning is necessary because there is no point in having this talent or uniqueness if you are not going to use it. It is like telling Pavarotti not to sing. Part of his fulfillment and appreciation of his talent comes from sharing it with the world, bringing joy to others as well as to himself. Not sharing your talent could be like having money in the bank but not using it. The only way your purpose can truly come to life is by sharing your uniqueness.

Discovering your purpose is only the first step; the path onward requires hard work and dedication. That is why the third eye is so important; it helps you keep your actions in check, staying aware of your personal journey to attain your purpose.

You may have to undergo some trying times, but if your head is focused on the end result, a bit of discomfort on the way will be worth enduring.

> So, what brings you to life? Remember, finding the answer may not be easy.

The Long Journey Ahead

On your journey to embodying your purpose, you must understand a few things. The first and a very important point is the fact that there is not just one single way to live your purpose. If someone's purpose is to heal others, their options range beyond becoming a doctor. There are many ways that one can heal others. They can become a nurse, physiotherapist, an expert in alternative medicine, a spiritual advisor or pastor, and the list goes on. It does not matter what road you take; just make it your own.

Many will be misinformed and believe that, once they find their purpose, smooth sailing ensues from there. But this is far from the truth. Discovering your purpose provides only the first step, and the road can be difficult. It is great when you find your purpose because it gives you direction, but that does not mean all the pieces will fit together so easily like a puzzle. Expect the road to be bumpy.

It is important to realize two things about your purpose. It neither has to be a charitable cause, nor does it have to sustain you financially. Your purpose can include selling the beautiful paintings you have created. At the same time, your purpose can include volunteering at your local orphanage during your free time. You can have a regular job, but on the side, fulfill your purpose. There is no strict format for how you follow it, as long as you follow the calling.

Another misconception suggests that one must undergo a devastating experience to truly find themselves. Not true. In fact, some people as children had a passion and knew exactly what they wanted from the start. Others discovered what they wanted from various jobs and life experiences. Not everyone must undergo a life-or-death situation to discover their true purpose.

What other misconceptions are out there? Well, let's continue. Many people believe that the only way they can make a real difference is by having the title, power, or authority. But this is not the case. Look at remarkable characters such as the Rev. Martin Luther King Jr., or Mahatma Gandhi; neither had formal authority, but both went on to do great things. It is not about having a title; it is about having the drive.

Overall, you need to understand that purpose takes time. It is an evolving process. Most people are not born knowing what they want from life. They take it one step at a time; they undergo various experiences, and from these experiences they come to terms with what they love and hate. It is important to put yourself out there and try new things. Otherwise, you will never really know for sure what you do and do not love.

Many people believe that age limits purpose. That if you do not discover your purpose by your early twenties, you are doomed to live a purposeless life. But let me tell you this: Purpose knows no age. Many individuals did not reach their ultimate potential until quite late in their life; if it was not too late for them, then it is never too late for you. Consider the example of Colonel Harland David Sanders who went through many travesties and difficult times, until he found his calling much later in life. All it took to start was a special recipe for making fried chicken (he finalized it at the age of 49), which later became one of the most famous food chains in the world, KFC.

At times, you may look back at your life and think, "I have wasted so much time; if only I knew what my purpose was back then." But the truth is you are exactly where you are supposed to be. Each portion of your path helps you appreciate the current moment, or the moment when you actually do discover your purpose. Do not get so caught up in this idea of regret. Because if we spend all our lives thinking of what could have been, we will be blind to endless possibilities ahead.

Some people never step in the direction of their purpose because they feel they do not have enough experience or insufficient qualifications. Well here is the thing: If you keep doubting yourself and never step in front of the fire, you will spend your entire life thinking you are not qualified enough. Nobody is ever fully ready to take on their purpose head on; you do what you have to do and evolve for the better throughout the process. You have to begin. You are not going to be perfect and all-knowing from the start. So, dip your toe in; it's time to start moving.

Purposeful Leadership

"He who has a why to live for can bear almost any how."

\- NIETZSCHE

You cannot lead without a clear and coherent purpose. True leaders in all forms, whether they have authority or not, share one quality: **Purpose.**

Purpose serves to unify and strengthen a leader's sense of direction and, consequently, the direction of the system. Purpose motivates people in a unified direction and injects meaning into every contribution they make. For example, most of the time people at the lower rungs of the organizational hierarchy of a company are treated differently, and perhaps this treatment takes away from their motivation. But when a leader brings people together through shared purpose, everyone's job is clearly seen as essential to the success of the organization. Purpose unites, motivates, and clearly directs individuals. From the custodial department to the top management, everyone works toward one goal, one purpose, with all contributing.

As a leader, if you have purpose, less time is wasted on trivial matters, leaving more focus for the bigger picture, the why.

A leader without purpose is like a person lost in the middle of the forest, not knowing why he or she is there, and not having a compass to find the way back home.

Be the Purpose You Want to See in the World

"The two most important days in your life are the day you are born and the day you find out why."

- MARK TWAIN

Once you start to think in terms of purpose, your actions begin to change. You think before you react to anything, asking: Is this in line with my purpose? At what cost? Is it really worth it?

This focus will help you not only make better decisions, but also be less reactive in situations with heightened emotions. For example, imagine you've just finished a stressful work day and are stuck in a traffic jam, when suddenly someone bashes into the rear end of your car. Normally, this situation would initiate the reaction to fight, scream, and make a scene. However, if your third eye is activated, you will think in terms of purpose. Is this situation really worth making a scene? What would this fight cost me, in terms of accomplishing my purpose? When you give your brain just a few seconds to catch up with your gut instinct, you may be surprised at your calm response.

Purpose is extremely important to a business. Many businesses focus on making money and reaching targets. The key focus should not be only on making money, although money is essential for business, but also on igniting the business purpose. In our interdependent world, we look for purchases that enhance our quality of life and our survival. Every time we make a purchase with our hard-earned cash, we want to place our money in the most suitable products. If businesses stopped focusing on competition, focusing instead on providing people with products and services that truly add value to their lives, the whole business world would be transformed and life improved.

Purpose is about putting your unique talents, whether in business or on a personal level, in service to others. Purpose is about using your own personal contribution to push society forward. The first step is discovering what truly makes you unique. That discovery transforms into purpose when you discover how you can use it to move a system forward.

- For a blogger, it can be about bringing people together through reflections about life.

- For a wildlife activist, it can be about helping people connect their daily actions to saving the wildlife on the planet, and/or being a spokesperson.

- For a hairdresser, it can be about making people feel beautiful by cutting and styling their hair to show off their best features, express who they are, and where they are going in life.

- For organizations like Facebook, it is "to give people the power to share and make the world more open and connected."

- For Etsy, it is "to keep human connection at the heart of commerce."

- For Sony, it is "to be a company that inspires and fulfills your curiosity."

- For Google, it is "to organize the world's information and make it universally accessible and useful."

Now it's your turn. What is your purpose? If you already know it, are you following it?

"To forget one's purpose is the commonest form of STUPIDITY."

- NIETZSCHE

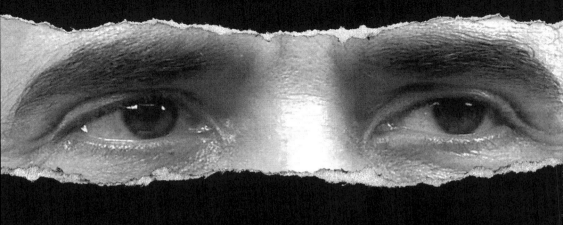

Whose eyes are these?

PILLAR II
KNOW OTHERS

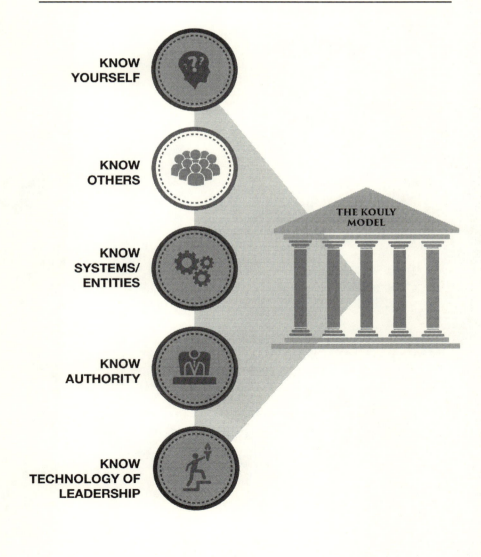

THE TEN EYES OF LEADERSHIP

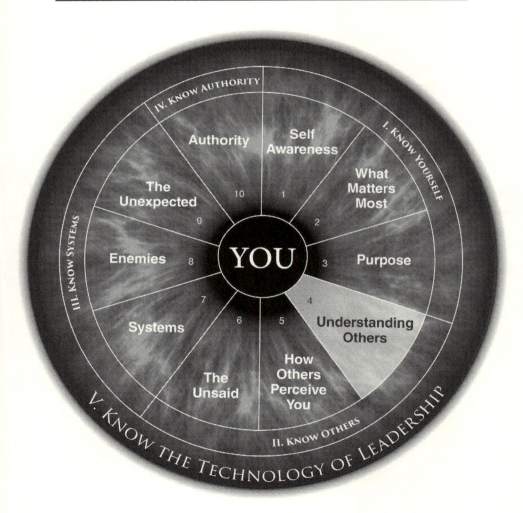

CHAPTER FIVE

THE FOURTH EYE: UNDERSTANDING OTHERS

"And those who were seen dancing were thought to be insane by those who could not hear the music."

- NIETZSCHE

I once heard this story from someone I truly respect, and it has resonated with me throughout my life.

A woman — let's call her Tina — went to the corner supermarket to buy her favorite cookies. She bought the cookies and headed to the park where she spent the day under the sun reading a book. In the afternoon, a stranger came and sat next to her on the park bench. Tina did not think much about it and continued delving into her novel. Then suddenly something caught her eye.

The stranger opened up her bag of cookies and started to eat one. THE NERVE! she thought. She looked at him, horrified; he had not even asked whether he could take one. Shocked and not really knowing how to react, Tina reasserted the cookies as her cookies, by looking at him and grabbing one for herself. The stranger did not even react; he just smiled and continued to eat. It became almost a showdown; he would take a cookie and so would she, until finally...the last one.

She did not move; she waited to see what his move would be. He looked inside the cookie bag, grabbed the cookie, cut it in half and gave her half. At this point, Tina was boiling. "He even took a piece of the last one!" she thought. Frustrated by the nerve of the man, she picked up her bag and book and walked away. As she caught the bus on her way home, she shuffled through her bag to look for some extra change. To her surprise, she found the cookie bag she had bought that morning. She could not believe her eyes. Feelings of embarrassment overtook her. The entire time she had been on that park bench thinking the stranger was eating her cookies, she had been the rude one taking his — and he allowed her to, with a smile!

Perspective can change in seconds, once you see the story through another's eyes. That is why judgment can be your biggest downfall — it can prevent you from seeing the truth and beauty within a given situation or person. Had Tina realized earlier that this stranger was actually showing her kindness, she would not have spent that hour judging him negatively.

"We judge ourselves by our intentions and others by their actions."

STEPHEN R. COVEY

Walking in Their Shoes

The fourth eye enables us to see the world through someone else's eyes.

Why is that point of view so important? To begin with, seeing through someone else's eyes allows you to let go of judgment, which can be very liberating to you, as well as to the other person. Understanding another's point of view and feeling with that person — empathy — tends to make you patient and forgiving. It is difficult to empathize with another without first, as the saying goes, walking a mile in that person's shoes. Trying to see the world through another's eyes gives us a new perspective on life, and on the beautiful things that our own eyes failed to see.

> *"You can't really get to know a person until you get in their shoes and walk around in them."*
>
> - HARPER LEE

It's Not Me, It's You

Have you ever been driving on the highway and someone zooms past you and you think to yourself, what an idiot that driver is, driving so recklessly? Now, did you ever, while driving, come up behind someone driving so slowly that you thought, this person must have nothing important to do in life? Maybe, just maybe, the reality is, in the first scenario, you are the lazy one and in the second scenario, you are the reckless idiot!

We always seem to have a good reason for our own behavior but rarely do we give others the benefit of the doubt. In other words, we credit their behavior to their idiocy while our behavior is due to chance or bad luck — that terrible situation we encountered. This difference is referred to as the Fundamental Attribution Error, and we all make it at least some of the time.

"When you judge others, you do not define them, you define yourself."

- EARL NIGHTINGALE

It is always easier for us to lay blame on another person. We see the same issue in relationships; when two people fight, each lays the blame on the other. "He just never gave me attention." "She never appreciated me." "He was always working." And the list goes on and on. The saying "it takes two to tango" should be ingrained in our psyches. Nobody is perfect... nobody. So, when a fight happens, instead of automatically laying the blame, try to understand the other person's position. Maybe you contributed to the way this person acted. Maybe not. Just hold off on the judging and the blaming, and try to be more understanding. When we stop focusing on our own perspective and see the other's point of view, a whole new world is revealed.

When we lay on the blame so strongly that we never consider other points of view, we end up generalizing and stereotyping everything according to our own limited understanding, and we see a distorted version of reality. Our generalizations and stereotypes are frequently wrong and almost always represent only part of the story.

> *"Everything that irritates us about others can lead us to an understanding of ourselves."*
>
> - C.G. JUNG

To Whom Am I Speaking?

Picture yourself starting your first day at work; you are nervous and you want to make a good impression. However, you enter the office without so much as a proper greeting and you start mumbling about all sorts of random things. You are so nervous and so focused on your own feelings that you do not even notice the confused expressions of those around you and you continue to mumble, then walk away hurriedly, still fixed in your own mind. It is not the best first impression, because from the second you started mumbling, you confused them, losing their interest and making them think, "What is this person going on about?"

What would work much better for you is to have your first and fourth eyes open and aware. Now picture yourself stepping into the office and being overwhelmed by shyness and nervousness. Since your first eye is aware that you are a shy person and tend to lose control in front of new people, your first eye will try to change your mindset. You will notice even from the first second that you are mumbling, and at the same time your fourth eye will notice the confusion in the people around you. So, to turn the situation around, you might say,

"Sorry I was mumbling. I'm just excited to be here, and I look forward to meeting you all." Simple and straightforward, because you know you get shy, but with the recognition of your feelings, you are able to be coherent. When we get too caught up in our own feelings and our own insecurities, we forget those around us and their reactions. So, it is best to be aware and catch yourself, as in the second situation.

Let's take it one step further. Brandon, who politically is a pure Democrat, comes to the office and starts up a conversation with one of his colleagues. Brandon gets on the topic of politics, not realizing his colleague is a Republican. If Brandon rambles on about how the Republican Party has messed up and only fools follow this party, his colleague may not react too well. After the conversation, Brandon may realize that his words are the source of his colleague's open reaction, and may notice the colleague now actively avoiding Brandon because he just does not like him.

This chapter is all about understanding those around you, being aware of their reactions, and understanding the reason behind these reactions. Had Brandon's fourth eye been open, he would have noticed the discomfort in his colleague's eyes and perhaps would have asked early in the conversation which party the colleague belonged to. That simple question, showing Brandon's interest in the colleague's point of view, could have prevented the tension between the two.

Without paying attention to the identity of the person you are speaking to, you will either lose the person's interest or end up unknowingly harassing the individual. The fourth eye takes into consideration all facets of the person and helps you bond and connect with them. The fourth eye is about having the genuine curiosity to understand the person in front of you, and respect the other person. You understand that, although they see the world differently than you do, that is fine, and you aren't threatened. Rather, the other person's point of view is something to embrace.

Where Are You Coming From?

The fourth eye allows you to see others' differences, understand them, and accept them. Understanding and accepting others' views is crucial when trying to survive in a community, because trying to impose your ideas on others can result in a range of reactions, from avoidance to a punch in the face!

We live in a multicultural and dynamic world. We all share the same humanity and capacity for love, but we differ in our worldviews, values, and priorities. The differences are what make the world so special. No two people are the same and we need to recognize and appreciate this, not try to change it.

Let's say you are a pacifist. Anything to do with war, you truly hate. If you talk to someone with a military background, who truly believes that sometimes war is a necessary evil to ensure safety, you cannot start by blatantly insulting his views. By doing so, you would insult not only his belief, but you would be indirectly saying that the years he spent abroad, risking his life on a daily basis, were of no value. You would insult this person on so many levels that, I am pretty sure, duck and cover would no longer be a drill! We each have our experiences that have shaped us and made us who we are. We each have our own journey and pace. There are many ways of seeing the world, each different, and we need to understand and respect the differences.

Let's take another, more extreme, example. It will be very, very difficult to convince someone who grew up in a broken home, beaten daily by his father and made to feel worthless, that people are inherently good. It would be a wasted effort. Instead, by showing compassion and understanding of his resistance and reactions, you may be able to demonstrate human goodness to him. By showing him love and not judging him, you may make more of a difference than talking at him or trying to convince him of your reality.

The fourth eye is about having compassion or knowing the other person well enough to know when to just listen and when to act. The question to ask yourself is: Why am I saying this or doing this? Is it to assert my beliefs or is it really to help or connect with this individual?

What Drives Your Behavior? What Motivates You?

The key to understanding others is to understand what is important to them. What drives their behavior? What makes them wake up in the morning? Let's go back to the story with you as the pacifist who appalled the veteran by criticizing the armed forces. Having established that he is a veteran, you can now consider the reason behind the black eye he gave you, after you suggested that the wars he fought had all been just a waste of time and lives. Is it because he fought bravely during his early days? Did he lose a lot of good friends? Is the reason for his reaction that he sacrificed so much to protect his country? Did you just push a button that insulted his entire being and worldview? If so, your fourth eye must have been shut, sealed and stapled closed, and your statement was more to get your own point across than to truly understand his view.

What motivates others is another way of saying what drives them. If you are a manager or head of a project and you want people to work harder, think of their motivations as the accelerator pedal for your project. You must understand what motivates your people at their core. Ask them questions such as what their dreams are, what they wished for in their youth, and what their aspirations were before the hardships of life forced them to turn another way. Each and every one of us, however much we age, has a little child locked away inside us. This innate kid defines our aspirations and indirectly sets our drive to move through life.

Your employee might mention art as something he loves; his fondest memories came from the late nights he used to spend painting his dreams on a canvas. Unfortunately, somewhere along the line, he forgot himself, forgot what he loved. By tapping into this motivation, his love, you may be able to rekindle his motivation. You might tell him to decorate his desk or the office space, so he feels more at home, or you might assign to him more of the creative endeavors. As a result, he will work better and achieve better results. But you won't know this option exists until you inquire, listen, and understand.

Whose eyes are these?

Where Are You Stuck? What Are Your Fears?

"The only thing we have to fear is fear itself."

- FRANKLIN D. ROOSEVELT

Leadership at its best is understanding where an individual is stuck and helping them move forward. So many things drive individuals. Unfortunately, fear can be one of the biggest barriers that we as individuals must overcome. We may know deep down what we are born to do, but another voice comes along saying, you are not good enough, you are not smart enough — the voice of the little saboteur inside us all. Being able to understand individuals' fears and setting them free from those fears can be one of the greatest acts of leadership, but it requires a great amount of attention from our fourth eye.

It all depends on where and in what the person is stuck. Are the issues easily remedied, or do these fears resonate at a deeper level?

For example, your co-worker might tell you she feels trapped in daily work routines and knows she can handle more complicated tasks. Unfortunately for her, she doesn't have the necessary academic credentials to be placed in a higher position. Telling her to go back to school may unlock a set of fears that she never dealt with properly. She may worry about whether she is smart enough, or too old. Maybe her household finances won't cover the tuition. But the alternative is for her to be trapped in a position she is not learning from. She requires more challenge for her growth. How would you motivate this individual? How do you help her overcome her fears? Humans like progress, and without progress there is no point in life. Thus, discovering what keeps others stuck is important.

The fears people have can be a massive roadblock holding them back. Fear can keep a person feeling trapped for quite a long period of time. Your co-worker's fears are holding her back from pursuing what she truly desires deep down. Feeling stuck and fearful can prolong unhappiness. Her fear may cause her to seem disoriented on the job, and lacking in focus. In no time at all, her performance could drop severely, showing why it is so important to get to know what fears hold people back.

How Do They Make Decisions?

As with the first eye, the decisions we make are not our own. Each individual is made up of voices that affect each decision they make. But it is not only the first eye that should be aware of these voices but also your fourth eye, in order to understand others better.

For example, there have been numerous stories that relate somehow to the following: A friend, relative, someone you know chooses to devote their life to medicine even though you know that they love to act and have a raw talent for it. You can tell this decision was not their own. In fact, it was the decision of their parent or an influential person in their life who always pushed them to be at the top of their class and to succeed in every endeavor. Their parent/guardian perhaps felt acting would not pay off and was not as prestigious as becoming a doctor. As we noted earlier, living the life expected by others stands as one of the most common regrets of the dying. Instead of judging your friend, you can make them aware of where the decision really came from, and try to encourage them to make their own decision.

Sometimes understanding comes down to just a matter of not taking things personally. Each of us has some baggage from our caretakers. Whoever raised us —mother, father, aunt or uncle — were not perfect and neither are we. Every decision they made resulted from the voices circulating in their own heads. So, if your mother ever picked up a slipper and hit you, it is not because she does not love you, but because that was how she was raised, and that is what she knows. It does not make her actions right, but when you start to view people in this manner, things become less personal. You start to understand what drives them, their motivations, and why they do the things they do.

This understanding is not easy; it requires your fourth eye to be wide open and aware. Understanding people is a task with many layers. We are all emotional beings, driven by our past experiences and sentiments; it is a grave mistake to think our actions are always based on rational thinking. Most of the time, we act based on our voices and experiences.

What Do You Value Most? What Are Your Core Beliefs?

"To understand the heart and mind of a person, look not at what he has already achieved, but at what he aspired to."

- GIBRAN KHALIL GIBRAN

Think about your core beliefs (e.g. 'equality', 'God', 'freedom of expression') and your values (e.g. 'family', 'preserving the environment', 'honesty'). Grab a pen and a piece of paper and jot them down. Now, take a look at this list and ask yourself: How much do these values and beliefs define me as a person? Your answer, I'm assuming, is going to be something like "a lot." People are basically characterized by their values and beliefs, and their behavior and interactions with others are driven by those beliefs.

Naturally, you think that these values and beliefs are the right and most important ones, and everyone should share the same ones if they are in their right mind. Not to burst your bubble, but that is simply wrong! People have different values and different beliefs, and that is okay, as long as the values and beliefs do not cause harm to others. That is the beauty of life. And frankly, people should accept and embrace these differences.

It is the job of your fourth eye to recognize that those around you do not necessarily share your beliefs and values, and you should show respect for theirs regardless. Being aware of these beliefs can also make interactions smoother, with less room for misinterpretations. Just to clarify, I am not talking about individuals who have extreme beliefs, such as terrorists who invoke harm upon others. I am just talking about the differences in perception of the world — how we were raised, certain customs. If any of these practices harm others or force them into situations against their will, this is another topic entirely.

"Our natural tendency is to project onto other people our own belief and value systems, in ways in which we are not even aware."

- ROBERT GREENE

Understanding the values and core beliefs of others will not only give you peace of mind, it will also allow you to exercise leadership more adequately. Understanding another's beliefs is like looking through the other's eyes, straight to their essence, and finally knowing why they do what they do. When you understand the other, you will understand what motivates them and use that to mobilize them and get the most out of each and every person. A leader is nothing without the people he needs to mobilize, so how can he not take the time to truly understand their intentions and motivations? What could be a better way to mobilize people than knowing their core principles in life?

Leadership is about mobilization. In order to mobilize others, it is imperative that you understand things like who they are. Are they females or males? What are their personalities like? Professions? Age group, are they young children or adults?

What drives their behavior? If you understand what drives their behavior, you can use it to mobilize them for your cause. Is love driving their behavior, fear, etc...

What motivates them? What do they wake up in the morning to do? What do they live for? These are all indications that you can use to motivate them further. What do they value most? For example, if many individuals value the safety of their families, implementing safety procedures or precautions will appeal to them, as they feel it is a need.

Where are they stuck? Are they continuously afraid of moving forward? or stuck in old assumptions or a need to please? A leader needs to understand and know these things to make a more impactful difference, to remove the obstacles that stand in their way.

How do they make decisions? When you are able to decipher how they make decisions, then you can reach them at the root, or know how to coax their decisions in your favor or toward your cause.

Without understanding others, leadership would be non-existent, or surely not as effective.

"Don't use your words to criticize, condemn, or complain; use your words to appreciate, inspire, and empower."

- DEBASISH MRIDHA

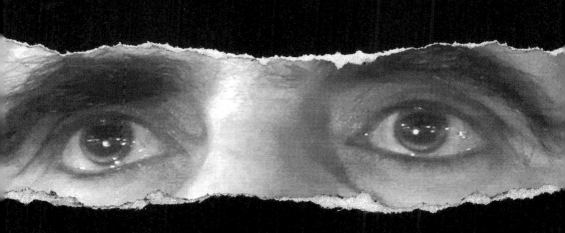

Whose eyes are these?

THE TEN EYES OF LEADERSHIP

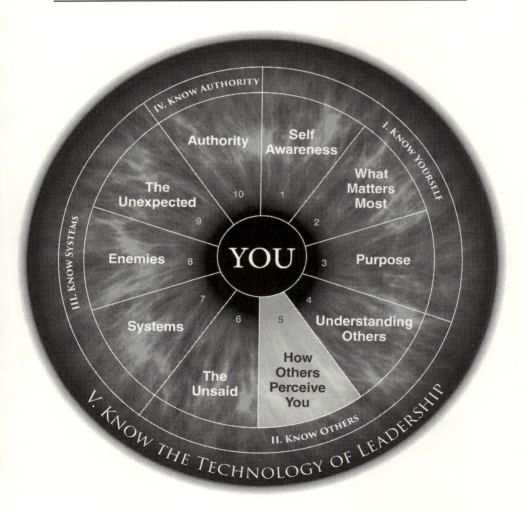

CHAPTER SIX

THE FIFTH EYE: HOW OTHERS PERCEIVE YOU

"The eye cannot see its own lashes"

- CHINESE PROVERB

I came across a funny story, which I hope you do not find inappropriate. I always refer back to it when talking about the fifth eye.

An old woman suffering from a gas problem went to see a gastroenterologist. "It is not really a big deal," she calmly stated to the doctor. "I don't know why my husband insisted that I come and see you. I'm kind of surprised that he knows about my bloating. Whenever I pass gas, it neither smells nor makes a sound. To tell you the truth, I can be in a silent room, a crowded elevator, and no one can hear or feel a thing. I've even let out a dozen since I've gotten to your clinic. You didn't know

I was doing it, did you? Well that's simply because mine don't smell and are silent," she said with a giggle.

"Hmmm," the doctor responded as he examined her.

He then handed her a prescription and asked to see her in ten days.

On her next appointment, the old lady exclaimed, "I don't know about the pills you prescribed doctor, but my gas stinks terribly now! However, I'm glad it's still quiet!"

The doctor responded, "That's good! Now that we've resolved your sinusitis, let's clear out your hearing."

We all have a natural predisposition to assume the way other people see things is very similar to, if not exactly like, our own perspective. "Of course, everybody wants to put on the air-conditioning, can't you see that I am sweating?"

Not only do we not see things as others do, we are also often in the dark when judging the impressions we make. **Our misconceptions can happen in two ways:**

1. We are unaware of people's signals, and automatically assume they see us exactly as we see ourselves (although even how we see ourselves can vary widely; some see themselves as perfect, highly agreeable and always right, while others believe themselves to be shy, unattractive, or barely noticeable).

OR

2. Though we manage to pick up some of the cues people throw our way, we fail badly at interpreting their meaning.

In both cases, we're toast.

This lack of awareness can be seen, at best, as naiveté. Unfortunately, lack of awareness can have extreme repercussions on our personal and business lives. The fifth eye is focused on understanding how others perceive us, in order to avoid these extreme repercussions.

Seeing ourselves through other people's eyes can be a very enlightening journey, if we have the courage to look at things in a different way. Besides, seeing yourself through others' eyes might actually save your life.

You Don't Want to Be Someone's Dinner

When drinking water, a gazelle keeps an eye on her entourage and carefully inspects the environment for any threat. Misreading her external surroundings will, to put it gently, compromise the gazelle's survival and growth.

Knowledge, or information, can be the difference between life and death... literally.

Just like this gazelle, humans are always part of a system (family, sports team, business organization, country, etc.). Also like this gazelle, humans are wired to be on the lookout for signs of danger and cannot afford blind spots. When threatened, they either run away, freeze, or roll up their sleeves and attack. In all cases, they send clear signals that they recognize the presence of danger. They are alert and may be ready to strike.

Failing to realize that a group we belong to perceives us as a threat can be very costly. As a famous Arabic saying puts it, "If you see the lion's teeth, do not think the lion is smiling."

The biggest mistake you can make and the deadliest threat to your survival and growth is to shut down data, either by blocking feedback, or by not properly using information you have collected. If you have information on a problem that others have with you, but are unwilling to address it, you are not using the information properly.

There should be few surprises in life; the system always sends signals. Still, it takes some people a divorce or a layoff to realize that the way they thought they were perceived by others was not really accurate. Whenever you are surprised by others' reactions, it probably means you missed, misread, or misused a lot of the signals they sent. Remember that unused data is useless.

How Accurate Is Your Radar?

People deal with us based on their own perceptions of us, not our intentions or our views of ourselves. Believing that you are highly tolerant won't make a difference if people see you as judgmental and fault-finding. The moment they are asked to work with you, they will react to you based on their own interpretations of you, not on what you believe about yourself.

As previously highlighted, everything that we say or do can and will be used against us. Our actions and words have an impact on the systems we belong to. While, many claim not to care about how others perceive them, deep down, we are all wired to want to fit in.

Being oblivious to how we come across to people is a recipe for disaster. Not only will our obliviousness impact our physical survival in the group, it will also affect our social existence. The quality of our relationships with our family, friends, and business partners is directly influenced by the way those people see us.

Think of it this way: How tolerant are you towards people who falsely view themselves as hilarious, and keep throwing offensive or bland jokes around?

No matter what reasons push us to behave in a certain way, people around us pick up on what we do, interpret it through their own eyes, and react to us according to their own interpretation. The more distorted your understanding of how others see you, the greater your risk of eventually being thrown out.

How's Your Love Life?

Do you love yourself? Our perceptions of what others think of us are often centered on our views of ourselves. Research shows that we rely on others' impressions to feed our preconceived views about ourselves. So, when we have low self-esteem, we are more likely to expect people to dislike us and criticize us harshly, and we may fail to notice that some may actually admire us.

Without awareness, we instinctively pay attention to the signals that reinforce the views we hold about ourselves. That's why ego and arrogance severely distort our fifth eye.

Recognizing System Glitches

When people say things to us or about us, they do it for a reason, and the reason isn't always us. When trying to understand how people perceive us, it is important to remember that everyone sees us through unique lenses reflecting their own stories, worldviews, and experiences in life. While some view nearly everyone as trustworthy and capable, others are skeptical of almost every person they meet until proven otherwise.

With our fourth eye wide open we can begin to understand other peoples' experiences, worldviews and stories. This will help our fifth eye grasp through what lens others are perceiving us. Their criticisms and reactions may have nothing to do with us but are an expression of how they perceive the world through their own eyes.

It is sometimes healthy to set aside others' judgments of us that don't match the way we see ourselves. Nonetheless, one should be cautious in dismissing the criticism of others, for there may be some truth in their judgment.

Failing to see the signals that people send, or wrongly interpreting them, constitutes a serious glitch in our social awareness that will have an impact on our survival and growth.

When a colleague frequently leaves the room as soon as you enter the meeting, or vehemently throws in an opposing idea for every one of your propositions, chances are there is an unresolved issue that you need to address. Failing to notice this pattern or misreading its underlying message will worsen the dynamics of your relationship.

If people frequently withdraw from you in social gatherings, it is unlikely to be merely a twist of fate. Look for an underlying reason; you're probably coming off as dull or disagreeable.

In a very different example, if higher management struggles to remember your name despite your major contributions in highly profitable projects, this may be a red flag that your work somehow comes in under the radar so that you never get the credit you deserve for it.

Expanding Our Perception

Have you ever attended a long technical seminar where you felt that nothing would be better than taking a long nap at that very moment? You look around to see the sulking faces of colleagues sitting next to you. Some are asleep, others disengaged, while others are making a genuine effort to keep up with the seminar. Among the fifty attendees, probably the speaker is the only one with absolutely no clue of how gruesome the presentation is. As he introduces "Slide number 256," you secretly wish he could experience his speech from your seat, having to listen to his monotone voice accompanied by his tedious, endless slides.

This is what the fifth eye is about.

The fifth eye allows you to scan your environment and accurately read signals (words, body language, behavior, etc.) that others are sending, and then interpret them (understanding whether the others are engaged, angry, or bored).

The fifth eye will bring to your attention the nuanced differences between how you view your delivery and how others perceive it. Someone who always cracks jokes might think that he is the funny one in the group, the one with a sense of humor, always lightening up the situation. However, others may regard his jokes as offensive sarcasm, or as a sign of an unserious mind. Yet, while finding his anecdotes inappropriate or simply not funny, they still may laugh so as not to make him uncomfortable.

You Are So Funny I Could Kill Myself!

Sharpening your senses and developing your understanding of how others see you are critical to your survival and growth, because people try their best to fake it, and for good reason. Who knows how many times you walked away thinking you made a great impression when in fact you bored people to death? An accurate reading of others' reactions to you will prevent you from perceiving the polite laughter which disguises discomfort or boredom as a genuine sign of being amused.

We must learn to develop our fifth eye's reading skills, because the way people react is not always clear or visible. You may have the potential to be a brilliant salesman, but if you are unaware that by talking way too much and too fast you leave people drained, you will never get ahead professionally or socially. You may see your clients' desperate nodding as a sign of approval, but if you take a moment to put yourself in their shoes, you will probably recognize their struggle to keep up with your monologue.

We have been trained to fake and sugarcoat our interactions with others, first because we want to come across as pleasant; and second because we don't know what our honesty might cost us. Many people believe that bluntly sharing their thoughts will put them at odds with everyone around them. Therefore, people are rarely blunt and direct with us, but we really should recognize the sugarcoated response. As much as we claim to have a big heart that welcomes all kinds of feedback, being regularly subjected to the harsh and aggressive truth is tiring. (Remember Jim Carrey's movie Liar Liar? If you don't, I suggest you check it out.)

Ask yourself:

- Am I able to detect emotions on others' faces and understand what they feel?

- How difficult is it for me to interpret others' responses to my behavior or words?

- Am I often confused by why individuals react to me as they do?

Look Around

A good way to study others' reactions to you is to weigh them against their normal reactions to other people.

For example, if you go to meet with a certain potential client in his office, and you always notice that he remains seated in his chair behind his desk, and rarely maintains eye contact with you, you may feel a bit uneasy about what he thinks of you. But your concern might increase if you also see that he greets your competitors warmly, meets with them in an informal setting, and cordially walks them out.

What does his behavior say about his view of your potential business? By reading the signals he sends, does he seem to value your presence as an asset to his company or as a liability? Is it possible that he has some personal issue with you? Is he acting this way on purpose to keep you on the defensive? Are you a threat to him, and he is trying to undermine your power?

With awareness, it becomes clear which interpretation best suits your case, but it is important as well to look for patterns in the person's overall behavior. Be careful, however, not to base your conclusions on one impression. After all, we are humans; we all have our off days. The key lies in understanding the motives behind a person's reaction, both for your own survival and your growth in business and in life.

> **Watch for patterns in your interactions with others. Gradually, you will notice that their reactions to you are often consistent.**

Calibrating Your Moves

Do you know how your co-workers perceive you? Do you really?

Are their actions in line with how you believe they perceive you? If you want to change their perception of you, what areas do you need to work on?

Do they see you as an asset or as a liability? Are you an enemy or an ally? Are you scoring points with the system, or losing?

Data from our fifth eye enables us to see ourselves through

other people's eyes so that we are aware of the system's feedback and reactions to what we are doing and saying, and can make corrections accordingly.

The fifth eye observes facial expressions, body language, tone of voice, and the spontaneous answers to our questions and interactions. The fifth eye helps us pick up data not only when someone is present but also through their emails, phone calls, and behavior in meetings.

After observing our environment and gathering data from our surroundings, the fifth eye invites us to reflect on what we are observing and what people are telling us.

Once we become aware of how people perceive us, we will be able to understand or expect how they will respond to our actions in the future, and be able to adjust our behaviors accordingly.

Keeping our fifth eye open is critical so that we don't keep making the same mistakes — or missing out on opportunities.

We must train ourselves to regularly ask questions such as:

- Where did I mess up? What could I have done to leave a better impression?

- Is my shyness leaving an unfavorable impression? Do people perceive me as conceited or disconnected?

- Do I put people at ease? Or am I too worried about what people think of me? If so, does my worry give the impression that I am condescending or self-centered?

- Am I easily approachable or do I make people feel judged?

Retuning Your First Eye to Your Fifth Eye

Research shows that personal awareness is a good indicator of our social awareness (D'Amore & Skolnick, 2008). A young man who sits sloppily and is unaware of how his posture impacts his status in the system, will probably be equally unaware of how others view him and what they say about him. A young woman who does not take care of her personal hygiene will fail to perceive how her bad breath pushes people away, and will most likely be totally ignorant of how others see her.

Conversely, when we are conscious of ourselves and learn to pick up and regulate our own emotions, thoughts, words and actions, we are more likely to be in tune to other people's reactions to us.

The more we develop our first and fourth eyes, the more our fifth eye is refined.

Our first, fourth and fifth eyes must work in parallel at all times. When used together, they expand our perception and complement each other, maximizing our chances of survival and growth. When I get upset, my first eye will notify me of the emotions that are boiling in my chest, and the way I am shouting at home and acting aggressively. My fourth eye, on the other hand, will pick up the anxious glare on my wife's face, informing me that she is getting scared of my behavior. If my behavior becomes rooted in a pattern, she may start perceiving me as a stressful partner or a potentially abusive one. My fifth eye will pick up on her passive-aggressive behavior the next day, and infer that there is a good chance she remains upset from my behavior the day before.

Whose eyes are these?

A Double-Edged Sword

Juggling the information from the different eyes requires time and practice, as it elevates our awareness. Using the information requires balance, being able to correctly weigh the data your eyes pick up. The key is to filter the information and learn to find the right balance. You can't allow yourself to get overwhelmed by the first eye's data flow, missing out on all its signals. Neither should you over-analyze others' perceptions of yourself, becoming hostage to their approval.

The purpose of the data that our eyes collect is to increase our awareness, and inspire us to give up dysfunctional behaviors affecting our standing in the system. The fifth eye should never be about nervously tracking what others think about us, trapping ourselves in social anxiety. If the fifth eye hovers in a constant state of alarm, we may never get away from feeling awkward.

Self-awareness pushed to the extreme becomes a double-edged sword. Scrutinizing others' reactions to us may become paralyzing. Awareness is more about balance than control; control breeds perfectionism and unrealistic expectations. Too much worrying about how others perceive us will eventually inhibit our behavior and suppress our spontaneity.

> **The purpose of awareness is to enhance our survival and growth; awareness is never about trapping ourselves in our thoughts.**

You Are NOT the Center of the Universe!

Having your fifth eye open should not produce paranoia. It is neither reasonable nor healthy to assume that people's reactions to you are always and only about you. Here, the fourth eye is an important companion to the fifth. When you interact with someone, many influences come into play, shaping the signals they send. For example, a person who woke up on the wrong side of the bed may be physically tired, or may be preoccupied by a hundred different things not even closely related to you. One person may act edgy or in a rush not because he or she is bothered by your presence, but because they are late to an important appointment, or simply needs to go to the bathroom.

Look at the reactions people have, without bias and without jumping to conclusions. Look for repeated behaviors and patterns to make sure you are not mistaking someone's mood swings for a conscious and deliberate reaction to you.

Ask yourself:

- What exactly did I notice? Stick to the facts. Refrain from analysis at this stage.

- What would explain his or her reaction toward me? (Brainstorm possible reasons.)

- Is the reaction toward me really about me? If yes, what can I do about it?

- Does his or her reaction toward me have more to do with him or her than with me? Are they projecting?

- Could the cause be other people, events, or things not related to me?

- Is this behavior limited to interaction with me, or does this behavior extend to others?

- Is the reaction toward me about who I am as a person or about something I did? Is there anything that I can or want to do about this?

After going through these questions, it is up to you to decide whether you think something needs to be changed or not.

More Factors Are in Play

The impressions we leave on others also depend on how compatible our personality is with those surrounding us. If you are naturally loud and cheery, you probably create a less positive impression on someone who is calm and sensitive to noise. If you are an introvert who dreads small talk, you might come across as reserved or arrogant to an extrovert. You're likely to make a better impression on those who are similar to you. Those who crave approval and work hard to accommodate the needs of others usually leave good impressions with everyone, but the extreme form of this personality may compromise the person's own needs and wants in the hope of pleasing others.

The possible factors do not stop there. People's views are also shaped by the setting in which they meet you. Someone who meets you after you just went through a painful breakup will most likely not see your light and chatty side. Their views of you also depend on the role you play in their lives at that specific time. For example, employees will treat a boss differently from the way they treat a colleague. The attitude toward their boss stems from an entrenched relationship with authority (Chapter 11 will further emphasize this point), but with their colleagues it is usually a less formal relationship.

Calling Additional Fifth Eyes to the Rescue

With practice, our fifth eye will become so embedded in us that we will be able to pick up signals left and right. With exercise and time, we will be able to distinguish when someone's distant look is simply absentmindedness, or whether their behavior has something to do with us.

However, as much as our fifth eye is developed, we will not be sure of how we come across to others unless we have the humility to recruit additional fifth eyes — other people — who will nourish us with accurate data from our environment.

In my corporate career, I surrounded myself with a team of well-trusted people acting as my fifth eye. They knew exactly what to look for, whether in negotiation meetings, corporate gatherings, or even during mundane workdays. They always kept me aware of how the system felt towards me so that I could make corrections when needed. "Everyone is watching you; it's better to keep a low profile," or "You are not visible enough; the board doesn't even know the project was your idea. Be more visible," or "Despite the public support for your initiative, there is actually a lot of resistance behind closed doors."

The Trade-off Between the Bliss of Ignorance and the Ugly Truth

Feedback is always challenging to accept, but is the key to progressing.

How open are you to feedback?

How do you behave when someone is about to share a candid opinion of what others think of you? If you're constantly irritable and defensive in the face of potential criticism, people will easily sense your defenses going up and will likely avoid sharing anything with you. Similarly, if you burst into tears over a slightly negative appraisal, your colleagues might simply choose to avoid the drama in different ways. Some will not share feedback at all anymore, while others might fabricate white lies to avoid an uncomfortable situation.

Narcissism and ego can only make things worse: Not only do people with narcissistic tendencies have their fifth eyes seriously skewed, but they are also immune to any type of feedback. They are living with a time bomb. One day, reality will hit them. Hard.

As much as we try to hide or deny our vulnerability to feedback, our emotions are easily perceived by others. When people are worried about our reaction, they will tread lightly when revealing their true feelings about us, if they say anything at all.

Burying our heads in the sand is certainly less nerve-wracking than enduring long, candid feedback sessions. Refusing to listen may leave our feelings unblemished by others' harsh views of us, but staying in the dark and continuing to act the way we always have, **will guarantee two things:**

1. People's perceptions of us will remain the same and might even change for the worse.

2. Closed eyes and covered ears will definitely not lessen the impact of any blow coming your way. Don't act too surprised when a ticking bomb lands beside you!

Besides, when you block feedback, you are shutting away both the good and the bad, conditioning people to lie to you. When someone lies to your face about your negative reputation, how can you be sure that they are not lying when they praise you?

Helping People Help You

Creating a setting that allows for open and honest dialogue is essential; so is choosing the right time, place, and people to ask for feedback. Make sure the person giving you feedback knows that you're sincerely interested in learning how they perceive you. Explain that your goal is self-development and awareness. Revealing some faulty characteristics of your own may break the ice and help you get honest answers. (Be careful: Honest answers may not be the ones you want to hear.)

Genuinely invite people to highlight your major blind spots in the system's perception of you. Encourage them to signal you when your delivery and interventions are not perceived positively by others, even when it comes to your strengths. We often fall into the trap of over-delivering on some of our assets, turning them into weaknesses. Through honest feedback, we will know when being vocal becomes too loud, or when being honest comes across as rude.

Remember that you are asking for feedback to improve your image in the system, NOT to explain yourself, blame others, or get into arguments. If you hear something you don't like, welcome it and then thank the person who said it. You can decide for yourself whether it is something worth working on. But since you have access to all this data, why waste it? It is a sincere, precious gift that can make you a better you.

> **Smart people build enough support structures and create an environment where it is safe to share feedback.**

Breaking the Spell of the Powerful and the Beautiful

Even when you invest the energy and time to create a suitable setting for feedback sharing, you may still find it hard to get people to hit you with the ugly truth.

When you are in a position of authority, it is tricky for your staff to tell you exactly what they think and feel. There is too much at stake, and the price of being an honest fifth eye can seem too costly.

This problem is not limited to bosses. Studies show that people with abundant resources (money, connections, power, intelligence, looks, etc.) must devote extra effort to developing their fifth eye. When these people fail to let others know they want relationships founded on honesty, they can easily slip into believing they are nearly perfect, especially if everyone around them places them on a pedestal. Those with power are usually surrounded by flatterers (Yes-Men) interested in accessing their assets. To get an honest opinion, they have to insist on its importance and reassure those around them that they will not be reprimanded.

> **When someone is too impressed or intimidated by your presence, it will be hard for him or her to react honestly to you.**

Leading with the Fifth Eye

The way others see us matters not only for survival and growth purposes, but also from a leadership perspective. Knowing how others perceive us plays a very important role in how we exercise leadership.

Without the awareness of your fifth eye, you could wrongly believe your employees are fond of you and appreciate your management style, when in fact they aren't and they don't. Imagine your surprise when you get a collection of transfer requests on your desk. Even governments understand the critical role this eye plays, which explains why nations invest so much in intelligence and information services.

When we do not pay attention to how the system perceives our words and actions, we unconsciously leave room for faults in our leadership. We receive signals from others constantly; ignoring the signals shows either complete heedlessness or self-absorption to the point of not caring. Yet care is at the core of leadership. How can we mobilize people if we cannot project a caring and serious presence in their lives? How can we expect our interventions to inspire if the other person is unimpressed, disengaged, or even worse, feels threatened? Failing to see ourselves the way others see us will hurt our interventions and ability to mobilize, because our impression on others counts.

> **Remember: You are constantly being watched and judged.**

Expanding Our Fifth Eye

The moment we change our focus and step into the third-person point of view (he did this, she said that), seeing ourselves from the outside, we start leading better lives. **The following list of questions will help us understand how others perceive us, enhancing our fifth eye's acuity.**

- What does the body language of others portray?
- Are they avoiding me?
- Do they behave differently toward me than toward others?
- Do people often react in a similar fashion when dealing with me?
- Are their behaviors in line with my expectations and

perceptions of them?

- What signals from the system could I be missing?
- Are my actions spreading a sense of comfort within the system?
- Are others absorbing what I am saying?
- Do people I interact with feel empowered after being around me, or do I leave them with negative sensations?
- Do others look forward to being around me, or do they try to politely avoid my presence?

Feedback Questions to Ask Others

These questions can help you understand how others see you. When you are ready to ask these questions, look for people you know will answer truthfully and thoughtfully. Asking these questions takes nerve, but if you are ready to grow, the answers can be quite revealing and uplifting.

- How am I an asset to your life? A liability?
- Does anything in my behavior seem like a threat to you or negatively affect you?
- Is there anything I can do, or stop doing, that would improve our relationship?
- How do you feel working with me?
- Am I helping you? How? What specifically do I do that helps your performance?

- Am I standing in your way? What specifically do I do, or how do I do it, that holds back your performance?

- What have you learned working with me and what would you like to learn?

- Do you believe I am supportive of your success? If so, how? If not, why?

- What do you want from me that you are not getting?

- What's one thing you'd like me to stop, start, or continue doing that would help you be more effective?

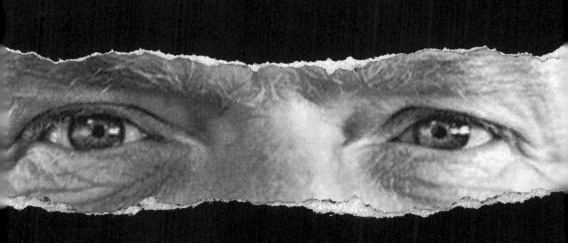

Whose eyes are these?

THE TEN EYES OF LEADERSHIP

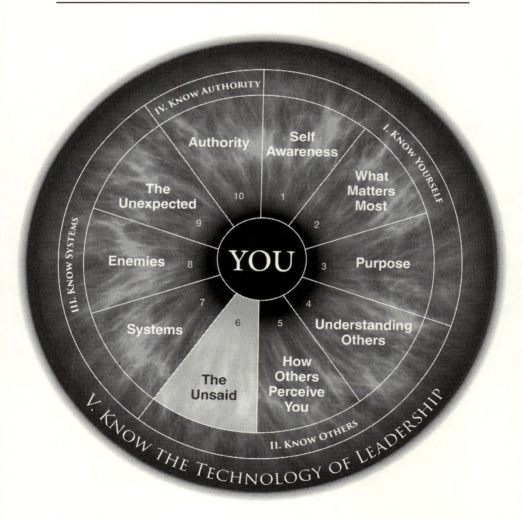

CHAPTER SEVEN

THE SIXTH EYE: THE UNSAID

Sitting with her arms crossed and reclining in her chair, the woman seemed disconnected from the rest of the group. Although she chimed in with opinions every now and then, and drew a smile on her face, nobody paid enough attention to the things she was not saying.

When she left for the day and never came back, the office felt like clockwork with a gear missing. Some projects were stopped cold; others raced in useless circles. The news article about the suicide quoted her shocked coworkers, "We had no idea! It was a complete shock. She was a good worker, and always seemed so happy."

When your sixth eye is open, a person does not have to say everything for you to know how they feel. When your friend who is usually chipper and optimistic walks in with a plain smile, you automatically sense the shift. How about the person who claims everything is "all right," but you know it isn't? The unsaid covers a wide range, from reading between the lines of what is said, to body language, to noticing shifts from someone's usual behavior.

Since people are social beings, communication is essential to maintaining healthy relationships with others. However, a significant part of this communication lies in the vast world of the unsaid. For you to survive and grow, you must read between the lines and pay as much attention to the unsaid as you do to the actual words uttered.

> "The most important thing in communication is hearing what isn't being said. The art of reading between the lines is a lifelong quest of the wise."
>
> - SHANNON L. ALDER

You need to be present and focused to pick up the hidden messages lingering in the realm of the unspoken. By opening your sixth eye, the eye focused on the unsaid, you will easily discern those implicit hints suggesting a much bigger story behind what is being said.

Ways to Develop Your Sixth Eye

Begin by eliminating or reducing distractions. You are shuffling papers, paying attention to the blinking light on your phone, remembering the gift you need to buy for your mother, and trying to keep up with the conversation your colleague just started. We are only humans. Yet, in today's world, we all find millions of directions to attract our attention, so we stay distracted and our attention soon retreats from any one thing.

Being able to listen to the unsaid requires you to tone down or remove any distractions that might get in the way of your ability to focus on the whole person. These distractions can take the form of external disturbances (noise, clutter, interruptions) or internal diversions (personal prejudices, biases, mental preoccupation, hunger, lack of motivation). Anything that might interfere with your attentiveness should be addressed. Multitasking here is a formula for failure.

> **The unsaid will fall through the cracks if too many distractions stand in the way.**

Building Rapport with the Speaker

Imagine cracking a dirty joke in front of someone who is extremely religious and conservative. How do you think this person will respond? It is safe to say that person will retreat from you like a turtle into its shell.

Know your audience. The more you listen to the other person, the more respect you show, and the more likely the person is to speak directly and openly. When you build rapport with the speaker, you will be more sensitive to the signals sent, and hence more likely to hear the unsaid.

> **If you want to read between the lines, you must first understand and have some kind of connection with the speaker.**

Making Silence Your Friend

You are stepping into an interview for a highly sought position. You are sweating bullets and more nervous than you have ever felt before. In an attempt to appear interesting and confident, you never allow a moment of silence and you want to prove yourself so badly that do not even wait until the interviewer finishes his/her question. Consequently, you end up rambling on about nonsense. You become so caught up in your speech you miss out on all the blank looks the interviewers are giving you.

People hate awkward silences and jump in to fill the gap with reactive responses or random remarks. Silence is not that bad. It can teach you a lot about the other person or the dynamics of your relationship. Furthermore, instead of projecting confidence, when you need to fill every silence, it shows the opposite. Not being able to sit in silence stems from a deep-rooted insecurity with yourself, for within the silence you can hear the judgment of your own thoughts. All you need to do is turn on your sixth eye and try to decipher the messages left unsaid.

Noticing What the Body is Saying

Leaning forward and touching your arm are classic small signs the person is interested in you. Leaning backward with crossed arms and a stern expression could indicate defensiveness. You need to be able to tell the difference!

Reading body language plays an important role in your

survival and growth. This talent is a collaboration of your fifth eye (how others perceive you) and your sixth eye (the unsaid); the synthesized data illuminates the bigger picture.

Watching for Clashes Between Words and Tone of Voice

A husband comes back from work very late again, although he promised his wife he would be back for dinner early. As he opens the door carefully, expecting her to be waiting and perhaps yelling, he is taken aback by the silence. He sees her in the kitchen cleaning up the dishes, and she refuses to look at him or pay any attention to him. When he asks whether she is okay, she responds with, "Everything is fine," in a harsh, unwavering tone.

Suddenly remembering that he forgot their wedding anniversary, "I am sleeping on the couch tonight," he thinks.

Whenever the content of the conversation does not match the tone of voice, it is time for you to summon your sixth eye. There is often more to the story than what is said aloud, especially when the words used do not fit the tone of voice.

Tuning in to Your Intuition

Your heart intuitively knows when something is off. Pay attention to the physical and emotional responses of your body. If you notice any discrepancies between what you think you should feel and how you actually feel after a conversation, then something is not right. This is the time to start investigating hidden messages and agendas; your feelings indicate veiled information.

For example, you are negotiating with a prospective client trying to close a deal. At a certain a point during the negotiations, your intuition starts picking up conflicting messages. The client is still engaged in the negotiation verbally, but you pick up signals that indicate their eagerness to close has dropped. This could mean numerous things, including the fact that they may have received another enticing offer from your competitors. It is important for you at this point to catch their attention and make sure that you can seal the deal. The sixth eye makes you pick up on these subtle hints that could mean the difference between almost closing a deal, and actually succeeding.

Another example would be if you are trying to lobby support for a leadership initiative and your intuition picks up signals that an ally, who is openly supporting you in front of others, is shifting alliances behind closed doors. The sixth eye may pick on the subtler differences in their actions; perhaps they no longer are acting the way they normally do — they can no longer look you in the eye or shake your hand as firmly as they used to.

Furthermore, diplomats are, in principle, experts in picking up and interpreting the unsaid, because the words and the gestures in the world of diplomacy are loaded with different meanings that are not necessarily openly stated. Also, they usually deal with individuals who do not have the same language, so their sense of intuition must be sharpened.

Being the Master of Questions

You should not try to play a game of Twenty Questions, or feel that you are in an interview trying to unearth as much information from the individual as possible. But asking the right type of questions can reveal a lot of information — not only the information the person actually speaks, but also body language and circumstances, which reveal more of what they are trying not to share.

To help your sixth eye decode the unsaid, you must try to understand what questions the individual would be willing to answer. Be careful, however, and don't overwhelm the person with too many questions just because you want to know what they are reluctant to announce. Too many questions will have the opposite effect, forcing the person to be defensive and cautious when speaking to you.

For example, imagine if you were to tell your chairman that you want to shut down part of the company's operation because it is taking a hit and losing a lot of money. So, your chairman tells you, it is really up to you, as it's your operation. But you sense from many unsaid signals he is hesitant about your plan. So, with your sixth eye open, you start to inquire further as to the motivation behind his hesitation. Only to discover that there is a general shareholders meeting coming up within a week and it will look bad for the chairman and the board of directors to declare that an operation is shutting down. So instead, you decide to postpone the move tactically, just temporarily until the meeting is over. You need to be aware of the sensitivity of the situation to determine the best times to ask questions indirectly or directly, and the right questions to ask to gather information.

How Often Are You Truly Present in Your Conversations?

Active listening requires you to be present. It demands effort and patience, but it yields rewarding and worthwhile conversation, along with a treasure trove full of potentially valuable insights from your sixth eye. Here are some strategies for active listening.

Strip away the subjectivity

Listening objectively sounds a lot easier than it actually is. It is critical to get rid of your own judgment and biased personal perspective when you listen. Listening, by definition, is giving attention to what the other person has to say. Focus on capturing the messages first; you can process and interpret according to your own thoughts and perceptions later. It may help to consider how they are feeling, this is where your fourth eye (understanding others) can help. When you understand where they are coming from it may be easier for you to stay objective.

Don't interrupt

To make a conversation with someone smoother and more fruitful, allow the other person to finish his or her point before jumping in with conclusions or showering the person with questions. Don't interrupt and cut off the train of thought. After the person completes the idea, you may then ask questions for clarification or carry on with your interpretation or what you want to say.

Don't think about your next move; it is not a competition

A conversation is not a competition. You are not playing a game of chess; plotting what to say in response to someone's idea or opinion will do no good for anyone. Stay focused on what the other person is telling you. This will allow you to focus on the unsaid (e.g. body language, tone, hidden messages), attending to what they are saying and what they are leaving out. Listen and pay attention instead of plotting.

Listen to what is being said, not to what you want to hear

Often, we only listen for what we want to hear. We already have a belief or viewpoint in our minds, so we filter out what we don't like, accepting only what supports our perspective. Listen to what is really being said; perhaps it will shed light on the other person's perspective that you never considered. You need to hear the statement, truly listening and trying to understand it, even if you don't like what you're hearing.

Ask yourself:

- How present am I in conversations?
- Am I focusing on my next statement or am I listening to what the other person is saying?
- Do I try to listen objectively or do my own prejudices, opinions, thoughts etc. intervene?

- Am I paying attention to their body language, tone of voice, feelings etc.?
- Thinking back to my daily conversations, what aspect of active listening do I need to work on?

Active listening helps you be present and aware of your surroundings.

"Sometimes a cigar is just a cigar"

- SIGMUND FREUD

We can get caught up in reading too much into situations, which can be just as dangerous as missing unsaid signals.

"To go beyond is as wrong as to fall short."

- CONFUCIUS

Your sixth eye should neither stand in the way of you trusting people nor should it stop you from believing they are giving you the whole story. Sometimes, with some people, what is spoken is all you need to know. There really are no hidden messages. No need to be suspicious. Do not overanalyze what they say, and do not question every word they use — such suspicion will prevent you from listening and being present. Sometimes you just must take someone's words at face value, because it is sincerely what they mean. The trick is to know when and with whom your sixth eye can relax and take a nap.

> "Some people become so expert at reading between the lines they don't even read the lines."
>
> - MARGARET MILLAR

Balance is the Key

Being alert and checking for hidden messages has its uses, but so does not placing too much weight on them. You will need a balance between being aware and sometimes just letting things go; there is great value in both. For instance, if you are aware of hidden messages and their implications, you will always be ready for what is to come; few things will take you by surprise. You will be able to understand clearly why people act in a certain way and you will plan your actions accordingly. On the other hand, if you simply take words for what they are, disregarding hidden messages, you will live a simple life with less stress and worry.

There is also a downside to both strategies. You do not want to be too naïve, letting signals go right over your head. At the same time, you don't want to be too suspicious and over-analytical. Be on the safe side; find a balance between the two.

> "Fortunate, indeed, is the man who takes exactly the right measure of himself and holds a just balance between what he can acquire and what he can use."
>
> - PETER LATHAM

Neglecting the Unspoken

Have you ever wondered why someone was mad at you? Did you ever feel like it came out of the blue? Did they send signs you just did not see?

The importance of the sixth eye is highlighted when one considers the repercussions of neglecting the unspoken. To begin with, sheer disappointment will hit you when you expect someone to act a certain way and they don't because you failed to read between the lines. Not to mention you will probably feel confused and a bit naïve. You might also miss out on opportunities because nothing explicitly shouted, "Hey you! I am an opportunity. You should seize the moment before I hit the road!"

Another repercussion of neglecting the unspoken is false hope and misinterpretation. One step further is when you read between the lines, but you don't read correctly. Some people will undermine relationships with people dear to them by ignoring the unspoken words between them, and failing to keep a healthy connection. An example of this came during the U.S. elections of 2016, when most of the media and think tanks had predicted that Hilary Clinton would have a historic victory. However, this ended up being a misinterpretation of what the voters really wanted. It could allude to a gap between what was visible and obvious, and the underlying currents that dictated the direction that the country would take.

> "Intelligence is not expecting people to understand what your intent is; it is anticipating how it will be perceived."
>
> - SHANNON L. ALDER

What You Leave Unsaid

> "It's less the words they say than those they leave unsaid that split old friends apart."
>
> - FREDERICK BUECHNER (GODRIC)

You may be aware of what you say, but are you aware of what you suppress? The sixth eye also makes you aware of the words you leave unsaid. If you intentionally send hidden messages, make sure they are being received. When you tell a story, are others hearing what you want to convey?

> "There is no time to leave important words unsaid."
>
> - PAULO COELHO

We sometimes allow fear or insecurity to stand in the way of revealing parts of ourselves. Make sure that the things you leave unspoken do not haunt you in the future. We all have agendas. When we communicate with others, there are things left unspoken on purpose, to shield us from being vulnerable or because we are plotting something. Yet, no matter how hard we try, our intentions are usually exposed; it is very difficult to keep them hidden.

> *"No mortal can keep a secret. If his lips are silent, he chatters with his fingertips, at every pore."*
>
> - SIGMUND FREUD

Reading Between the Lines in the World of Business

As leaders, it is essential that you understand who your allies are and who your enemies are. Understanding what is not spoken can help you differentiate between those who are on your side and those who are aligned against you. These unstated messages are crucial. The more in tune you are with your sixth eye, the clearer other eyes become.

Activating the sixth eye is particularly important in the workplace. With the help of the data provided by the sixth eye, leaders can improve their decision-making, build stronger relationships with associates, and sort out problems more efficiently and promptly.

Consider contracts, for instance. The terms of agreement between two parties are not simply what is written down; the real agreement is more about the clauses that are not written, which is where the lawsuits usually nest! For example, some business contracts fail to mention changes such as what would become of the fees for the services if the exchange rate fluctuated — will it remain the same or be adjusted?

Interpreting what is obvious and acting upon it is not enough in the world of business. For someone to excel, set an example for others, and grow in a system, he or she must decode the unspoken language, being able to exit a meeting with information beyond what was actually said. Such a person will get to know more information about a candidate in an interview than the information presented on a resume. Another example would be organizations that live by many unwritten rules. For example, although the rules state that you can dress casually, if you were to show up in sweat pants, the glares alone would force you to abide by the hidden code, or stand out like a sore thumb.

Seeing the Unsaid

How aware are you of the unsaid? When was the last time you took a deeper look at your conversations? These are key questions each person must personally answer. The sixth eye not only acts to reinforce other eyes, but also contributes to overall survival and growth. The sixth eye can be tricky, but once you have mastered it, you will be able to read not only the lines, but what is between and beyond them as well. Sometimes you can call in reinforcements to make sure that you are reading the signs correctly and not missing something. Getting feedback from others is always a good way to check how open your eyes truly are.

"Quite often it's not about what is said, but what isn't. And even when it's spoken, read between the lines. Listening with the heart is just as important as hearing with the mind."

- T.F. HODGE

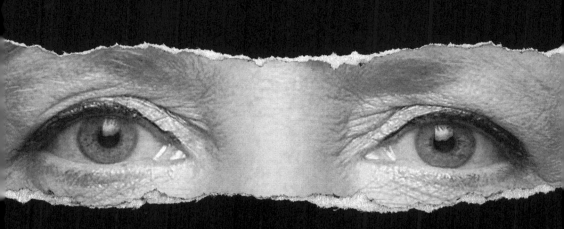

Whose eyes are these?

PILLAR III
KNOW SYSTEMS/ENTITIES

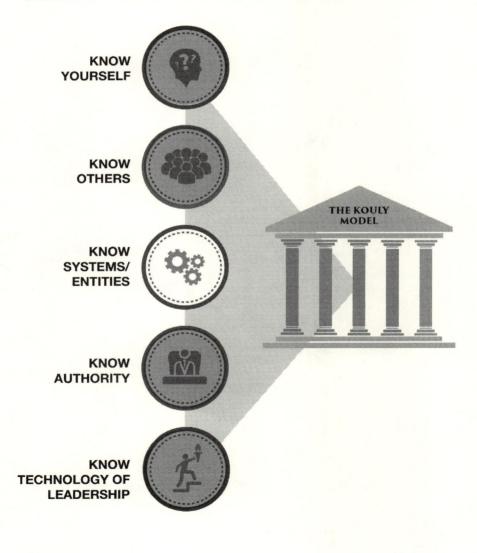

THE TEN EYES OF LEADERSHIP

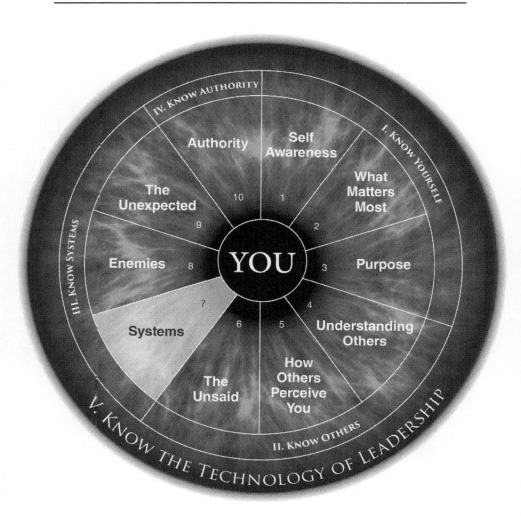

CHAPTER EIGHT

THE SEVENTH EYE: SYSTEMS

Do I Call You Dad or Boss?

Jake had his future set from the moment he entered college. Like his siblings before him, he knew he would go to work in the family business. When he turned sixteen, he started to feel the pressure. His summers were filled with internships in his father's company, and he worked in all the different departments to get a feel for how every aspect of the business ran.

The day Jake graduated, his father beamed with pride; for it was not only his graduation day, it was also the day Jake would finally take over the position in the company that was waiting for him.

Jake was optimistic and excited, but much to his surprise, it was not all happy days ahead for him. When he started to officially work for his father, he saw a different side of the man. He did not recognize this person. His father was short-tempered, bossy, and incredibly tense. He wanted things done and he wanted them yesterday! When Jake wanted to recommend something or suggest something new, his father would give him one look and that would be the end of the conversation. What Jake found to be the hardest part to adapt to was the fact that, when they were back home, his father went back to acting normally. They would joke and there would be a lot of affection. Nobody else in his family acted weirdly or ever talked about this difference; it was as if it was normal and accepted.

Jake struggled to get used to this hardest aspect of his work. At work, his father would not defend him or take his side. Jake felt continuously out of place and a bit shocked. Everything seemed to Jake like a personal attack, as if his father did not love him enough, respect him, or think he was worthy. His biggest problem was accepting that, at work, his father was a boss, and just a boss. All his personal expectations had to be checked at the door the second he walked into the office, because his father at that moment saw him merely as an employee.

Jake's father understood something very important that Jake still had to learn: Each system that we are a part of has its own specific purpose with different roles rules, laws, and protocols. If his father treated Jake like a son at work, and gave him special attention and projects, the employees who had been working there for years, who had much more experience, would start to feel resentment and would lose faith that they were being treated fairly and being recognized for their efforts.

Jake's father treated all the employees equally and wanted them to earn, not just be given, their positions. He understood this was best for the company, and the best way to move the business forward. If he showed blatant favoritism, mayhem would ensue. Jake's father is a good example of a person whose seventh eye is open. He was aware of which system he was in and followed the protocols of that system while he was in it. His family time was just that, family time. His work time was hard work.

Systems are extremely important; understanding that they exist and what they are like is crucial. Any set of elements that work together as part of an interconnected network is a system. Systems can range from an object such as a car, which functions as a result of its own internal systems, to parts of the body, such as the digestive system or the nervous system.

As an example of a system, look at the whole human body. It is made up of organs working together to keep the person living and breathing. The organs should work in coordination; it is this collaboration that defines a system. If one of these organs is in critical condition or is suffering from some kind of ailment, the result could be the endangerment of the whole system, even its termination.

Another example of a system is an ant colony. The ants hurry to their food-gathering tasks through a system of tunnels. Imagine one ant that does not comprehend how this system works and what its duties are. It will end up lost in an endless set of passageways and might become some bigger insect's food.

For the purpose of this book, a system means a group of people working together for a specific purpose. A company is a system, as is a basketball team, an alumni group, a country, a syndicate, or even a family of two. We are born into some systems and, as we grow up, we leave some and join some.

But we are always part of many systems simultaneously. We never deal with each other individually, no matter how much we want to believe that this is true. We deal with each other as part of a system. Normally, a child will react to his father as the system (in this case, the family) requires. An employee will approach his boss in a staff meeting differently than he will when playing pool after work, even if they are best friends. The dynamics of the relationship between two people takes on a different shape depending on which system it is operating in.

Take some time to consider:

- What are the main systems that I am a part of (i.e. work, home, society etc.)?

- Which systems matter the most to me?

May I Join You?

None of us can escape being part of a system. Even if you decide to seclude yourself, living alone on an island or in a cave, depriving yourself of some basic human needs, you remain part of a system: Nature! (And you will need to remember those survival skills you learned in the scouts.) However, if you do decide to join systems made up of people, some of the many needs you will be satisfying are:

- **The need for inclusion.** The desire to join others and be accepted by them. The need to belong.

- **The need for protection.** We have a need to feel secure and protected. For example, you never scuba dive alone; because, if something were to happen to you, at least you would have someone else to help. We are stronger in systems as we have more support and less risk of being harmed.

- **Our Basic Needs:** We need to feel that our basic needs are being fulfilled, for survival is more guaranteed through systems. Why are African refugees risking their lives by the tens of thousands to illegally cross the sea in overcrowded boats, many often drowning in the process? They are leaving because they want to be part of a system that fulfills their basic needs. In systems, in general, ensuring basic needs like food, shelter, and water is more reliable. We discovered a long time ago that, when we are together, we hunt more efficiently, and have each other's back. Some systems provide these basic needs better; that is why immigrants flee for protection and even the lure of a better life. For example, illegal Mexican immigrants who try to cross the American border seek better opportunities.

- **The need for affection.** Systems attract us because they can meet our desire to like others and be liked by them, and provide access to support structures and attention.

For us to fulfill our ultimate purpose of surviving and growing and satisfying basic needs, we must understand systems and their dynamics. We cannot survive and grow if we do not know the systems we belong to and understand how they function.

More Than Just Vegetables

It is important to recognize that a system is a whole entity; it has an identity of its own apart from the identity of its individual members. A system is not just a list of its members, but rather the synergistic effect of the interdependent relationships among those members, where "the whole is greater than the sum of the parts," as Aristotle stated. Take, for example, a salad. A salad as an entity is not tomatoes and cucumbers and lettuce and lemon juice. It is the combination and mix of those ingredients acting to become something different and grander than the individual elements. Change one of those elements and you get a different salad. When any component of a system changes, the group or system itself will also be altered.

Can You Survive in Chaos?

Another fundamental attribute of systems that one needs to know to survive and grow is that every system has its own rules, norms, patterns of behavior, and methods of feedback. If one is not acquainted with these patterns, the system will simply exclude him or her, or not respond to efforts at leadership. **The three major components that define a system with people are:**

1. **Formal structures:** Organizational charts, bylaws, etc.
2. **Cultural norms and forces:** Folklore, rituals such as casual Mondays.

3. **Default behaviors:** Response to conflicts, response to criticism. For instance, does everyone point the finger and blame each other, does the boss openly give feedback about work done, or is the system a sinking ship and nobody is saying anything?

These three components define the functioning and operation of a system and suggest whether it is running smoothly or is about to fall apart. Understanding these three components sheds a light on the inner workings of the company and its purpose. It is important for each part of these three components to match the purpose of the system. Just like people, systems dislike confusion and seek to avoid conflict.

Imagine a company that had no rules, no bylaws, no rituals, no vision, etc. At first, that might sound like a fun and free-spirited place to work. But then you would start noticing the utter chaos and lack of direction. Nobody is held accountable for anything, nobody knows where he or she is heading or whether to expect to be fired, and no one is reprimanded when stabbing someone else in the back.

People cannot live in chaos; it is unnatural. All these structures are in place to enable each person to understand his or her role in the organization, and to explain to each member of the system how the system functions. For example, rituals such as a company celebrating employees' birthdays or Sunday lunches with the family are forms of interaction that show a close-knit group. The rituals may seem insignificant, but if they are positive, they create a space for the parts of the system to bond and build trust. No system can function very long without cohesion and trust among its many parts. Hence, rituals such as Secret Santa or office celebrations can create more communication and trust.

To better understand a system, one must analyze the behavior and interactions of its elements. The elements are always communicating and interacting. Feedback, whether positive or negative, is accumulated, and that feedback can help or hinder the progress of the system. Even the absence of behavior is a method of communication; something is being said even when absolutely nothing is being done. For example, when a wife chooses not to reply to her husband's comments (absence of behavior); she is giving him the silent treatment, which is a form of communication. She is conveying that she is upset or angry and her husband (we hope) picks up this message as a departure from normal behavior.

You Are Not YOU in a Group

Have you ever seen a soccer or football match that has gone awry and wondered why? The game starts out wonderfully; each member of each team is cheering for their side. Suddenly, one person in the crowd insults another, and a full-fledged fight breaks out. No longer is the situation one of people enjoying the game. It turns into a tribal situation. Blue supporters feel they must defend any person wearing that color, and they lash out at every non-blue person who comes their way. What starts as a small misunderstanding between two people can result in a riot and some people may not even come out alive.

It is important to understand that people change when they are in a group . When the entire group is excited, this excitement automatically transfers to each individual and provides energy. Suddenly, you are just as pumped as the person next to you. The problem arises when everyone in the group starts to get angry, or has an excess of any negative emotion. When those around you get angry, you will automatically start to get angry; the reaction will hit you like a wave.

Violence and anger are accepted more in groups because there is more anonymity and less blame on each individual. Our most primal instincts come out when we know we will not be held accountable for those actions. One of the most important things to be aware of when you have your seventh eye (the eye on systems) open is to be aware of how you personally change when you are in the group. Have you become more violent? More passive? Excited? Each reaction can be part of the shared energy permeating the air.

Some groups become so unified that they forget to think as individuals. The problem with this is the group begins to think they are invulnerable, and they overestimate their capabilities and downplay their flaws. After all, many minds are stronger than one, right?

A second problem arises when the group views situations through a close-minded lens. If they believe they have been successful all these years due to the way they have always done things, they may shut off any alternatives to improve. In fact, they may look negatively upon any who try to challenge their ways.

The third problem is that uniformity becomes an obligation. If you are not conforming to the rules of the group, eventually you will be forced to do so, without even noticing that you were compelled, or how you were constrained. We are social beings. Therefore, we are extremely sensitive to any form of pressure, and we naturally want to fit into a group, to feel that we belong. So sometimes it is easier to just conform than to stand against the grain. This pressure is a common problem of groups. If the group's direction is dangerous or not well-informed, many problems can result down the line.

With one's seventh eye open, an individual can recognize when decisions are their own, and when they are influenced by the group. The individual will notice when an intervention is necessary to alter the direction in which the group is going. It is important for any group to be open to criticism, so it doesn't automatically fall into the herd patterns mentioned above. It is important for the individual exercising leadership to continually analyze two aspects of the system: What is being done and what is being said. If these two conflict, there is a problem that needs to be solved. This way of thinking can be similar to the workings of the fourth and sixth eye for the individual, but in this case, it is trained upon systems. Opening the seventh eye is very important to leadership because leaders must be able to craft initiatives with the system's inner workings in mind, and consider how the system affects individuals, their patterns, and their behaviors. By understanding these key elements, a leader can use the system's inner workings to leverage change.

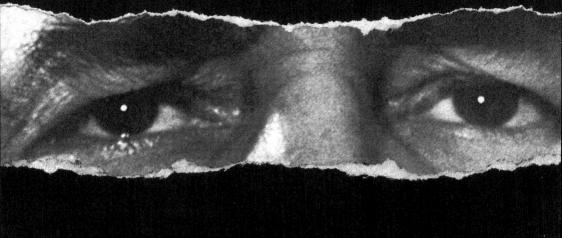

Whose eyes are these?

A Tricky Business Indeed

Systems are a tricky business. When you have your seventh eye open, you must be aware of everything that could prevent a system from moving forward. You need to stay aware of which aspects make it functional or dysfunctional. This is critical because you need to be able to assess properly where the downfall of the system arises. Leaders with their seventh eye open can understand how the system functions and grasp even the slightest of nuances. With this awareness comes great power, as you will be able to make better decisions about what will either enhance or hinder the system. For example, is everyone qualified to remain in the system?

If you have an orchestra, but the musicians do not know how to play, then you are in for some discomfort, noise pollution or whatever you would like to call it. Do the musicians in the orchestra get along? Or are they constantly trying to compete for the attention of the Maestro, or criticizing others in order to meet their own standards of perfection? Does the orchestra have a proper space to play and practice? These are all examples of questions that must be asked to understand the general functionality of the system.

Whether we like to admit it or not, sometimes the smallest nuisance can be a barrier to a system's proper functioning. For example, you expect employees to be productive and know their work requires close concentration and patience, but you have placed them in a hot and noisy environment. How efficiently do you think they will be in getting their work done? What about employees overloaded with work and projects? They will be so stressed they will not be able to function properly. With one's seventh eye active, one will be better able to anticipate potential mishaps and observe behavior like short tempers or rising error rates, as a sign that things need to be adjusted for the system to move forward.

Systems like simplicity; they like to know where they are going. The best systems are very cohesive; when danger arises, they aren't easily derailed. With most systems, however, anything resembling confusion or danger can create agitation that can cause the system to break into pieces. When roles or functions are not clearly stated or abruptly changed, when expectations are not met, members may begin to act out.

For example, if the chairperson of an organization calls for a meeting and then does not show up, what will happen? More likely than not, individuals will start to break off into small groups and chat, wondering why the person in charge has not arrived. After a time, they will leave, dissatisfied, and grumbling about their time being wasted. Even if they know why they were called together and one of them could potentially conduct the meeting and discussion without the person who was supposed to be in charge, no one may choose to do so, because it would go beyond the expectation of any group member's traditional or practiced role.

Systems do not like confusion. When there is confusion, instead of continuing forward, the members are likely to freeze, or run in the opposite direction. This clearly poses a problem: A group that is not cohesive, not working together, will never move forward. Most of the time will be wasted just trying to bring everyone together, and the real work will never get done.

Picture a battlefield. Soldiers who are not working together and decide to run off on their own will be the first to perish.

Those who stick to formation and hold together will most likely persevere, accomplish their purpose, and survive. A system will not function without cohesion. To have cohesion, danger and confusion cannot always be lurking around the corner. The system needs calm and order, a clear direction, and precise aim.

Systems also cannot function without purpose, and the pursuit of the purpose is never-ending; the purpose should be the driving force behind all the actions of the system. Without a clear purpose, the system will be irrational. Without a purpose, the system will resort to seeking purpose through traditions and old policies that may or may not make sense, but are at least familiar. "It is just how we do things around here." Without a purpose or a set direction, employees will blindly follow authority, never knowing why they are doing the things they do, or even thinking of a step that might improve an operation. Their only requirement is to be loyal and follow orders. Purpose mobilizes the masses because it paints a clear picture of why they are engaged in what they are doing; purpose gives them a reference point and guide. Hence, acts of leadership are continuously necessary to keep a system focused on its purpose. Leaders must know how the system is linked to purpose, and find ways to link initiatives and change back to an improved way of accomplishing the purpose.

Patterns That Can Destroy You

Mobilizing systems, however, is another problem entirely. Sometimes, a system will get stuck — in routine, in methods, in policies, in traditions. Some of the most successful companies plateaued because they believed their product no longer needed improvement. On a personal level, sometimes patterns start to form in a family, such as the father works late and the mother gets angry. If neither one wants to bend or adapt and both lose sight of the purpose (harmony), then the system will remain trapped and the parents will continually clash.

Being aware of the system's patterns is a major requirement for any leader, and the only way to be aware of the patterns is to have the seventh eye open. The seventh eye allows the individual to recognize where the system may be jammed. That recognition, with the support of the five pillars and the other nine eyes, can enable the individual to adjust the system to move forward.

Many times, systems have enduring patterns which the members of the system are used to, almost comfortable with. Change is equated to disruption and discomfort, no matter its intent. Trying to mobilize for change can be a very dangerous endeavor; those who benefit from the way the system currently runs will try to stop efforts to change at every step of the way. It is also difficult for any system (or person) to acknowledge the hard realities of a need for change. A system or a person will live in denial and make up excuses, rather than acknowledge and own any form of failure. So, the courage to mobilize for change requires the courage to face immense resistance to any efforts to shed light on the harsh truth. Truly mobilizing the masses requires linking change to the purpose of the system and ensuring that everyone knows how the purpose will be advanced.

Creating a Change

"Fur is murder," screamed the angry protestors who stood outside a clothing shop. Julie, who was among the protestors, was originally a quiet gal. She had never liked causing trouble, but always had a strong connection to animals. When she joined an organization devoted to saving animals, her animal rights beliefs were strengthened to the point of fanaticism. The group was so passionate about these beliefs that they maintained a strict vegan diet and no-fur-or-leather policies. Anybody who did not abide was expelled.

When Julie joined, she was enthralled by the passion and the drive of these people. Because of them, she had more confidence to stand up for what she believed, and even adopted new beliefs. Only a few months ago, Julie would never have had the guts to stand in protest with the rest of the group. But now, there she was, in the front row holding a poster depicting a murdered cow.

Group dynamics can sometimes push individuals to undertake acts of courage. Groups hold power over their members, and within each group there are always certain pressures forcing members out of their comfort zone to implement change. Had Julie joined a more destructive group (although this one was quite strict), such as a hate group, the group might have changed her in a whole other direction.

By herself, Julie might not ever have gathered enough strength to press for the change she wanted. But when she felt that others supported her views and were looking out for her, that thought gave her the courage to fight for something bigger than herself.

We are social beings; we have an innate need to belong, to be part of something. Groups offer a purpose and fill that need. When a group is going in one direction, the members feel more or less pressured to follow through according to the relative strength of their fear of isolation or seclusion. They want — they need — the comfort of belonging. Hence, a group with a good purpose is a strong force for positive change in the world. However, a group such as ISIS, which has been hijacking the news and aims for destruction, will have the opposite effect. Groups like ISIS have a harmful purpose, which has resulted in numerous murders and unacceptable behavior. Groups are powerful. The key is to inject them with positive purpose (in accordance with universally accepted values), so that the change they implement is helpful, not harmful.

Leadership in Systems

Systems without leadership cannot function. Leadership is essential to direct the system toward its purpose. When a system is off track, leaders must detect the veer, shake up the system, and re-route it. Without leadership, the system will either become chaotic or go completely in the wrong direction.

True leadership skills require one's seventh eye to be open so that the person exercising leadership is aware of the power the group has on its individuals. Furthermore, true leaders continually sense whether the group is heading in the right direction, and can figure out what actions are needed to re-direct individuals, and then the group as a whole, toward an alternative path.

Leadership is very closely associated with purpose: In order to exercise leadership, one has to clearly understand the purpose of the system in which one works. If a group is motivated by acts of leadership deriving from a strong purpose, it has a better chance for survival and growth and can contribute to the well-being of all.

To navigate the system and bring about purposeful change, you will need to frequently ask yourself these questions:

- Do I know and understand the cultures, default behaviors and formal structures of the systems I belong to?
- Do I understand the specific purpose of every system I am a part of?
- Do I understand the group dynamics that are affecting how the individuals in the system interact?
- What can I do to improve my understanding of these systems and its elements?
- How can I use my knowledge to bring about change in the system when needed?
- What lessons have I learned from previous conflicts with the systems that I belong, or belonged, to?
- How can I use that information to avoid similar conflicts in the future?

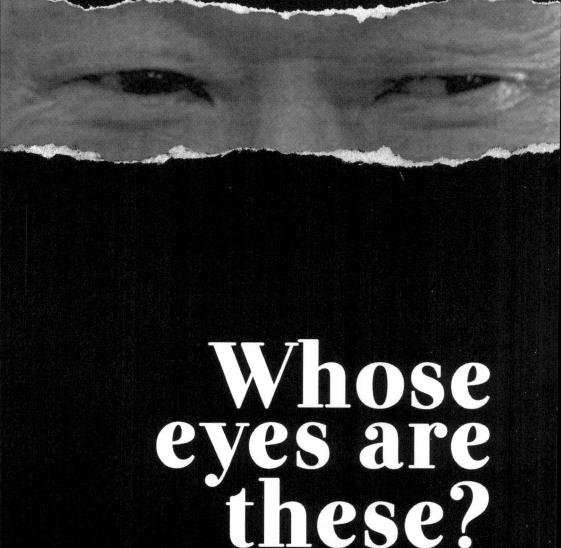

THE TEN EYES OF LEADERSHIP

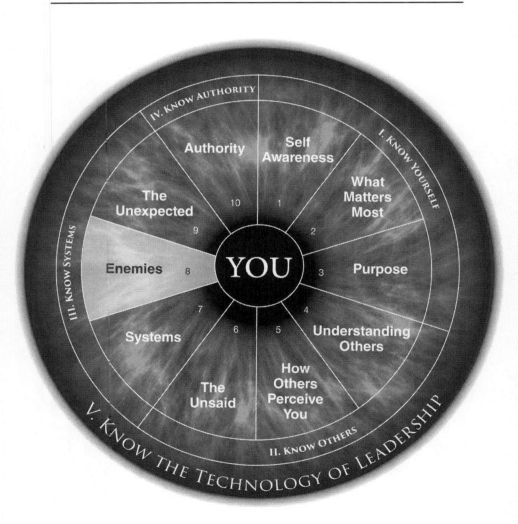

CHAPTER NINE

THE EIGHTH EYE: ENEMIES

"In the practice of tolerance, one's enemy is the best teacher"

– THE DALAI LAMA

Leadership Promotes Change, Change Triggers Resistance

We are social by nature, and as such we interact with people who carry different attitudes towards us. The quality of our journey in life and our exercise of leadership depends on how we deal with the people who populate our world. The spectrum varies from people who are neutral, to the extremes on both ends of support and opposition. For this chapter, we will focus on the different degrees of opposition that one faces in life, especially when exercising leadership. It can be a sensitive subject, and is quite loaded, but it is a subject of utmost importance and should be discussed.

Change disrupts people's equilibrium. Every time you introduce change to a system, you disrupt people's equilibrium in life. When you introduce change, you are shaking the structure and placing individuals out of their comfort zones. Leadership is needed when a change needs to occur, so more often than not, when you are exercising leadership you need to shake the system.

Once this change is introduced, those the changes favors will become supporters. Those the change does not favor will resist, because the change causes them loss, which is painful or threatening. The degree of resistance reflects the pain brought on by the change you introduced. Your enemies' resistance varies from passive resistance to active resistance, with people, or entities, lining up as opponents, rivals, competitors, antagonists and even archenemies.

For example, if you lead an initiative to introduce a change in an organization where machines will replace people, it is natural to expect that the people who will lose their jobs and suffer the pain of unemployment will view you as an enemy. What you are calling an act of leadership is threatening their entire existence, or an important part of their existence; your success would indicate their loss of livelihood. You are killing them professionally, so of course you are the enemy. They will express their emotions toward you like you are an enemy and they will do whatever is in their power to fight back. Enemy is a valid terminology because, in this specific case, it involves their livelihood. Imagine if one of these people were over 55 years of age; they may never be able to find another comparable job. How will they support their family?

Leaders often need to make such tough decisions, hence resistance is perfectly normal. But it is important to be aware of it. This is not meant to be scary, or heavy. It is merely a natural part of life. Although "enemies" is a loaded word, it is rare to find enemies who will go to very extreme lengths to hurt you (violence). But unfortunately, as history has shown us, sometimes they do, such as assassinations (e.g. Abraham Lincoln, Mahatma Gandhi, Martin Luther King Jr. etc.). Nonetheless, it is important for one exercising leadership to be aware of all the possibilities.

A friend once told me about his experience in top management and it changed the way I viewed resistance and my own management skills. In the early years of his time in top management, a few weeks after he was appointed as the national head of a global company, he called for an introductory staff meeting. As he had spent some time training his fifth eye (on how others perceive us), it was easy for him to tell right away who his potential supporters were, and who did not seem to like him much.

One executive made it his number one priority to go against whatever this man did or planned to do. It was clear that he was not on his side, but little did he know what he was capable of. Out of ignorance or inexperience, he overlooked the signals he was getting and decided to focus solely on the tasks he was hired to do. However, he soon realized that, no matter how much effort he put into advancing the operations and pushing his projects forward, something always seemed to be standing in the way.

The space he had given the individual, who viewed him as an enemy, allowed that person to rally a considerable number of people against him. Through malicious rumors and incessant lobbying, this executive managed to delay many of the projects my friend tried to initiate. The amount of time and energy it took him to try to neutralize the damage that was inflicted was immense. That story helped me understand the importance of staying close to your enemy, and the idea of the eighth eye came to life.

It's a Political Jungle Out There

Ancient history is full of stories of underhandedness and conspiracies. Misreading the intentions of a rival or failing to neutralize them or convert them into an ally, was likely to land kings and peasants alike in the grave with a stab in the back. While such life-threatening hostility may be more typical of ancient times, we cannot underestimate, even today, the danger that opponents or enemies pose and the risks of not managing them properly.

Think of how many times you proposed an excellent idea, only to have it shot down before it gets a chance to fly. Perhaps your colleague spread hurtful rumors about you, damaging your reputation and relations with the entire organization.

It is a fact of life that you will not be liked by everyone.

You are bound to meet individuals who don't really have your best interest at heart. You can decide to remain in the dark and choose to stay out of these political fights. However, the sad truth is that your enemies will still be out there trying to resist your initiatives. The most painful punch is the one you do not expect. Even governments try to avoid these surprises by spending huge amounts of money on intelligence agencies, carefully watching their enemies and even their allies, and spying to keep an eye on their secret activities.

Behind Enemy Lines

Whether in the workplace or a social gathering, the ability to recognize opposition and appropriately manage your relationship with rivals is essential for survival. The highly political nature of any system, whether a family, a building, a neighborhood, a syndicate, an organization, or a country makes it almost impossible to survive and thrive without learning and mastering the political game. Every one of us encounters a few rivals throughout the course of our lives. Most of the time, this results from an initiative they are against. Some people simply will dislike you for personal reasons, or have more rational motives such as the scarcity of resources, job openings, or opportunities. Whatever the motivation, your resisters are an important part of your life and cannot be ignored.

Why can't you just ignore them? Because they are intentionally working against you. Ignoring such an important and active force in your life and within the system can be a deadly mistake.

The eighth eye is an awareness tool dedicated to scanning for potential opponents and feeding you with crucial data about them. **The purpose of the eighth eye is two-fold:**

1. To keep you alive by knowing the strength, intentions, activities and plans of those who are against you. This awareness will allow you to take pre-emptive measures and protect yourself and your interests from any damage they could cause.

2. To make you better by giving you access to a wealth of feedback you can use to your benefit. Perhaps the resisters have valuable feedback to give.

The eighth eye is the eye focusing on all the countervailing forces that might undermine your survival and growth.

Where Art Thou, Enemy of Mine?

The word "enemy" can represent a wide range of people and manifest in varying degrees, from general resisters, to competitors, to opponents, to rivals, to enemies, to the extreme — your nemesis or archenemy. Not many people will have a nemesis or an extreme enemy, but in certain cases, they do exist. Individuals or corporations that will earn this title are ones that will go to extreme lengths to deter your progress.

For example, British Airways and Virgin Airways had what started out as a normal competitive situation. But British Airways altered this relationship when they actively interfered in the progress of Virgin Airways. They hacked databases to obtain customer information, called customers claiming that their flights were delayed or cancelled, and even went on to offer them cheaper flights. Luckily, Virgin Airways gathered proof of what British Airways was doing, and received a formal apology and compensation.

In general, however, most opponents are not necessarily enemies, in the common use of the term, or arch-enemies, but lesser degrees of one (e.g., competitor, rival, resister). Please note that within this chapter, the word enemy will be used interchangeably with other variations, such as resisters, competitors, rivals, opponents etc. There are differences, even slight nuances..

In corporate circles, enemies can be colleagues or seniors you have to work with whose intentions (thoughts or feelings toward you) and interventions (words or actions) are not in your favor. They resist the initiatives you come up with, sabotage your work, and strike down your ideas. This resistance can show itself in either active or passive campaigns. They resist your acts of leadership on different levels, from someone who merely objects to your actions (while remaining passive) to the 'enemy' who actively tries to stunt your plans.

An enemy can also be someone whose values you do not share, or whose actions cause you to fail in your own obligations. People who are competing for your resources also fall into the category of rivals, whether this be a colleague eying the same promotion or a competitor pursuing the same prospect. Sadly, more often than not your business opponents believe their success depends on taking away what you have (your customers, your resources, etc.). Instead of finding their own purposeful way to add value to the market, they make you the reference point and focus all their effort on undermining your projects.

In social circles, enemies can be acquaintances or "so-called friends" who work either publicly or secretly to harm you in one way or another. In short, an enemy is anyone who threatens your survival and growth and hinders your leadership initiatives. While this description of an enemy is very comprehensive, in no way does this suggest shooting at any moving target. Nor should you treat every enemy in the same manner.

And the Price Just Gets Higher...

Mastering the eighth eye is not only crucial to your survival and growth, it is essential in leadership work. Opposition — and rivals — come with the leadership package.

The essence of leadership is mobilizing people for a better life overall, although those closely enmeshed in any dysfunction within the system may not find the change an improvement. Mobilizing people can be a messy business demanding bold measures. Leadership interventions will not always be accepted or welcomed by everyone concerned.

Some of those who do not accept the interventions will be upset and some will take it personally. Some will smile to your face but internally will blame you, or in some cases, will gossip behind your back to undermine you and your strategies. Others will perceive your actions as a declaration of war, and will act as an army opposing your leadership efforts.

The bottom line is: You will face resistance in various forms.

Why? Because you never know until you start how displeased people will be. Even in a case where nobody is actually doing anything wrong, downsizing operations or taking a step, such as reducing the privileges of higher management, will always be unpopular with those affected. Similarly, if your leadership intervention is to promote transparency through blunt conversations in meetings, you will get resistance from those who enjoyed the life of a slacker, but now find themselves under the spotlight.

When you decide to get involved in leadership work, you had better have the heart and mind to face the resistance and resisting forces you will unleash.

The eighth eye will allow you to responsively manage your relationship with opponents. If done correctly, this relationship eventually will not only maximize the success of your own leadership intervention, but will also protect the system from potentially lethal strikes. The more power you have and the bigger the organization you are leading, the more resistance you must deal with, and the more danger you must anticipate.

A good example of the difficulties that can befall those who don't keep their eighth eye open was taken from the book *The 48 Laws of Power* by Robert Greene. Greene discusses the story of P.T. Barnum who, in 1841, wanted to purchase the American Museum in Manhattan to make a name for himself. Although Barnum could not secure the funds the Museum requested, he made a barter deal and a verbal agreement with the owners. However, at the last minute, the Museum sold its collection to the directors of Peale's Museum because of its strong reputation. To get what he wanted, Barnum walked the road of vengeance and sabotage. He launched a letter-writing campaign in the newspapers criticizing Peale's reputation and everything he stood for. The smear campaign worked, and the American Museum ended up selling everything to Barnum. Had Peale been more vigilant, his reputation may have been saved along with his business.

Blindsided by the Enemy

A great lesson learned from the Trojan War is not to let the opposition blindside you. The war between the Trojans and the Greeks lasted for a decade. Ironically, the move that put the Greeks ahead, the Trojan Horse, was packaged nicely, as a "gift." This gift left the Trojans dumbfounded. It was a gigantic wooden horse supposedly left by the Greeks as a tribute or a gift to the gods. Although some Trojans advised burning it, it was eventually accepted and taken inside the gates. Little did they know it was a hollow horse, filled with Greek soldiers, who attacked the city of Troy at midnight and won the war.

The eighth eye keeps your attention on the schemes your rivals might concoct, like a fire you wouldn't leave unattended until you knew for sure it was out.

So, what are the skills you must adopt in order to avoid being blindsided?

1. **Keep your eye on them:** If you know someone actively resists your initiative you need to keep your eye on them at all times. If you open your fourth and fifth

eyes, perhaps it will help you understand why they are acting the way they are. This will help you come up with creative solutions to help both the resister and yourself. If you cannot, it is important to be aware of what this person plans to do.

2. **Preempt any of their attacks:** You must continuously monitor them. As you watch, you can draw conclusions and make predictions about what is on their mind. If you feel that they will be scheming something, you will be one step ahead.

3. **Be prepared:** Neutralize or weaken them before they start. For example, if you know a colleague wants to stop your initiative, assume they may try to gain the support of your boss, even highlighting your mistakes to the boss, quite boldly. To neutralize the threat, you must speak to your boss ahead of time, and keep him/her informed during every phase of the initiative so that your competitor will not have a weapon to use against you.

4. **Engage your enemies:** Dialogue and discussion are essential to find common ground, where you can launch your initiative in a way that avoids causing them losses. Remember that the goal is the purpose or what you are trying to achieve with the initiative. Being able to reach your purpose by causing losses to the fewest number of people should be your goal. Just like in basketball, where your entire aim is to get the ball through the hoop, not to harm players from the other team. The only thing you need to do is neutralize opponents so they do not stop you from slam-dunking. It is important to interact with them, negotiate and try to find alternative ways

of doing things. By doing this, you can neutralize the impact they may have. Furthermore, as a leader, every act that you take must come from a place of empathy. It is never personal.

Are You Really Stuck in the Crosshairs?

As tempting as it may be to imagine that all your problems result from the deliberate attacks of an army of tormentors, not everybody who gives you a hard time qualifies as an enemy.

Look around. Who doesn't have an annoying co-worker or a temperamental neighbor? It is time-consuming and draining to deal with these people. However, most of the conflicts they bring to your life are not intentional. Many disagreements are a matter of varying perspective or working style, not a personal vendetta. With a bit of maturity and the right amount of self-control and awareness, you will be able to shield yourself from unnecessary frustration.

Not everyone who disagrees with you is Public Enemy Number One.

Enemies on the other hand, operate on a completely different level. They have their minds purposefully set to delay your growth and make your life difficult. The eighth eye helps you gather accurate data on your real enemies. The purpose of this awareness is to maximize your chances of survival and growth and make sure you are not building Don Quixote scenarios in your head and tilting at windmills.

There is a very thin line between being watchful and becoming paranoid.

Forget About One-Size-Fits-All Policies

Not everyone who disagrees with you is necessarily your enemy. Your opponents come in different forms and shapes. You need your eighth-eye radar to help you identify which is which. Building on the eighth-eye awareness, you will be able to choose the appropriate measures to handle your opponents.

You will need to be flexible and open enough to earn the trust of respectable rivals who are publicly against your initiative, but honorably come out and inform you in advance about their standpoint. It is natural to have people who disagree with your initiative. These competitors are to be treated with the utmost respect and valued as a source of information, as they will openly inform you about the problems in your initiative. Each piece of advice should be taken and used to improve your situation. You will also have to build up enough courage and resolve to be aware of co-workers from your team who resist you behind closed doors. You may also have to display enough compassion to forgive a one-time misfortune caused by an opponent.

This flexibility is important, because the motives of each kind of enemy may differ. Therefore, understanding their motives is key. This will require the use of other eyes, as stated before, such as opening your fourth and fifth eyes to understand the motivations and reasons why an individual is acting as they are. Perhaps if you understood the motivations, you can resolve the situation and remove the resistance. In the

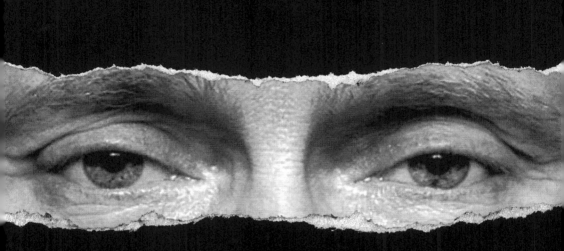

Whose eyes are these?

end, people are mostly motivated by circumstance, so when flexibility is possible, use it, if it does not compromise the initiative.

Most of the Time It's NOT Personal

I know it is easy to jump to the conclusion that "they just don't like me," or "they are jealous of me," or "they want what I have." But sometimes, it has nothing to do with you!

In many instances, those opposing you are not moved personally by who you are or what you say or do. They neither despise you nor wish you harm. Their focus is simply elsewhere — a tempting bonus, a nice word from the boss, or simply the pleasure of being right. You just happen to stand in their way. For them, if it were anyone else, they would do the same. It is not personal.

For example, what if you wanted to declare a certain plot of land a natural preserve, to protect it from poachers and anyone who wanted to cut down the trees. Automatically, you would have formed enemies, and not because they have anything against you personally. The poachers you would prevent from entering the preserve will not be too happy, nor would companies that need to cut down the trees to market lumber. They will be frustrated because they may have to look to other sources that may be costlier.

So, the second you take any action, resistance will always appear. But it has nothing to do with you; it is merely the fact that you have placed an obstacle in their way. If you stopped the initiative or if they were able to get what they want despite your initiative, they would no longer have anything against you. In this respect, it is not personal.

In other cases, people are against you (and your initiative) because what you expect from them entails costs they are unwilling to bear. This is particularly true because exercising leadership is about change. For instance, humans are avoidant by nature. We are prone to denial, especially in times of stress or pressure. We usually shut off what we do not want to hear and vehemently oppose things that require new effort. We will do anything to protect the status quo, and will find a thousand ingenious ways to withhold cooperation from a process we think is painful or time-consuming, especially if the long-term rewards are unclear.

Friends of Today, Enemies of Tomorrow

We, as humans, are tricky at times. Most people will support you when it benefits them. But the second you deviate from what benefits them or the path actually starts hurting them, they are out the door faster than you can say "Wait!" Unfortunately, relationships are not always consistent and stable.

Except for a very few individuals who have bonds with you that run deeper and have more layers (e.g. friends, family), the loyalty of your "supporters" is almost always conditional. Remember that your current supporters may at any point stand to lose something they value if your future interventions (behavior or words) no longer serve their interests. Their potential loss can be as simple as missing the comfort of things done in a certain way, or as serious as a lost job.

While scanning your environment for resisters and keeping your eye on the opponents you know about, make sure you also keep an eye on those you hurt (intentionally or unintentionally) on your way up. People who have been hurt find it difficult to forget. As Machiavelli puts it, "He who believes that providing new benefits will make great personages forget old injuries is deceived."

> The eighth eye also scouts people who might potentially become resisters.

When Too Much Resentment is Everywhere

You will also encounter rivals who are less rational and composed. When not kept in check, their anger, hostility, or chronic blame will likely divert your attention and drain your energy. Underneath their intense dislike for you and, many others, are deeply rooted issues and compulsions that have nothing to do with you. Without the awareness of your eighth eye, you can fall into the trap of trying to fix things, or get sucked into their attention-seeking games.

The consciousness of your eighth eye will allow you to discern whether:

- Their fight with you is a reflection of their own personal issues.
- You can convert these adversaries to allies.

- It is strategic to develop a rapport with them to build a reassuring relationship.

In rare circumstances, you may come across individuals who have made the fight personal and are determined to deter your plans. They are resentful, and resolute. In many cases, they are getting even with you for a past wound you have inflicted upon them (or they feel you have). When you have one of these people after you, **your eighth eye will sound the alarm and ask:**

- Did I do anything that might have prompted their offensive attack?
- Is there anything I can do to defuse their resentment?
- What can I do to watch my back?

In certain cases, you become the symbol of something they do not believe in; this is how assassinations occur. For example, the assassination of Abraham Lincoln resulted from conflicting beliefs and values. His initiatives to free African Americans stood in the way of many individuals who benefitted from slavery. His very existence threatened their way of life and, hence, he was assassinated. Of course, this is not the norm, but your influence and initiatives may very well threaten or challenge core values or positions others hold dearly, and the vigor of their defense of these may scuttle the best of intentions.

They Like Me, They Like Me Not

Your eighth eye helps you determine the intentions and

motives of your opponents. It is different from the fourth eye of understanding others because the intentions of opponents can be harmful. You not only have to be aware, but also very cautious. Clues exist, so carefully scan your environment. Be on the alert for signs of how your opponents relate to you in both private and public settings. What do they say about your initiatives? Do they use their resources (time, connections, money, and power) to defeat your ideas or to attack you personally?

Awareness and empathy are critical for comprehending the reactions of, and potential losses suffered by, your opposition. The eighth eye allows you to keep an eye on anyone suffering from a loss inflicted either by your leadership work, or by you personally. This awareness will call for preventive actions releasing the accumulated frustration and shielding you from harsh comebacks.

Without knowing what they want and why they oppose you, it will be hard for you to respond correctly to their conflict of interest. The eighth eye will inform you of whether the reason for your clash is just a matter of resistance, a struggle over power, or something far more personal and vicious.

Look around you with your eighth eye and consider:

- Whose short-term goals are not aligned with yours? How does this gap reveal itself in their behavior?
- Whose values are completely against yours?
- Who is fighting over your resources?
- Who stands to lose a great deal following your initiative?

- Whom have you deliberately or inadvertently hurt?

The eighth eye focuses on identifying those to be wary of and people who can be turned into a future ally. The eighth eye is about asking yourself:

- Is he or she a real threat or simply an irritating person?
- What does this person want? What are his or her intentions and motives?
- Is our disagreement personal, or do we just see things differently?
- What harm can he or she cause? How could this harm affect me personally?
- How can I shield myself from the damage he or she can inflict? How do I keep him or her from blocking my success?

Bring Out Your Magnifying Glass

The eighth eye is not about laying blame or passing judgment. It doesn't assume that your competitors are wrong and you are right, or that your opponents are bad and you are good. The purpose of the eighth eye is just to gather data and increase your awareness of some of the most influential people in your life.

Similarly, the eighth eye is not about giving in to the Machiavellian instinct. The data collected by your eighth eye is not to discipline, correct, or set up traps for those who oppose you. Rather, it seeks to inform efforts to neutralize them, so they don't obstruct your way.

Keeping your rivals on your radar does not mean deception or vicious paybacks. Dealing with your enemies certainly requires you to be wise and adaptive, but that doesn't in any circumstance imply that you should act unethically. Remember that care and compassion are at the core of leadership.

"Our survival and future are linked. Therefore the destruction of your so-called enemy is actually the destruction of your self."

- DALAI LAMA

Having Lunch with the Enemy

It is never fun to spend time with "the enemy," whether that means abusive neighbors or vicious colleagues. While you may believe it is safer to completely alienate yourself from these individuals, some of your resisters are people you'll need to exercise leadership and who will prove very useful to your personal and corporate growth.

Keeping the eighth eye open is about constantly tracking these people with your radar. Thus, it necessarily involves staying close to them one way or another. Try not to limit your contact to superficial greetings. Replacing brief hellos and goodbyes with actual conversations can prove to be very insightful. Regular get-togethers over coffee and meetings are essential rituals to gather the data you need. Keeping this proximity will allow you to closely study their body language,

Whose eyes are these?

watch their moves, and pick up the vibes they send your way. You can use this closeness to listen to their version of reality and gauge their reactions to your interventions. As much as you may wish to avoid being around them, train yourself to see these gatherings as learning opportunities and a way to test the waters.

The Perks of Having Them Close By

"Keep your friends close and your enemies even closer."

You may have rolled your eyes when someone used this cliché as advice, but you might be surprised by the benefits you receive from staying close to your enemies and keeping an eye on them. Competitors teach you great lessons in life and business. These lessons help you mature as a person and make you more resilient.

If you did not have anyone to compete with, how would you improve?

The dynamics of the tense relationship between rivals can generate a healthy competition, refining the skills and improving the interventions of both parties.

Think of people running for president. The stress of facing a worthy opponent often brings out the best in both contenders, each striving to polish his or her abilities and become better, while highlighting the shortcomings or wrongdoings of the other person. Threatened by the performance of the rival, each therefore works even harder to reach the goal. Now imagine there was only one person running for election. Why would he or she be motivated to work harder if there were no one to compete with?

Enemies build up our skills.

"A smooth sea never made a skilled sailor."

- ENGLISH PROVERB

Low-Cost Advisors

Even the most devious opponent can promote our growth without even knowing it.

When our friends and followers fear to share their honest opinions about our work, raw data from our enemies can shed light on areas that need improvement. The intensity of their dislike, and the time they dedicate to surveying every single move we make, means they are extremely well-informed about us. Why bother hiring a consultant when you can get the advice for free?

Our enemies are our best free-of-charge consultants.

Imagine you bought a new house. If you ask the opinion of people who like you or are neutral to you, they will probably give you acceptable feedback such as, "It looks great!" "Congratulations," etc. But if you ask an enemy, or anyone who already has a negative attitude toward you, the feedback from that person will most likely include the smallest details about cracks and imperfections that other people may not even notice. But remember, there is a kind of opponent who says the opposite of what he or she feels. Your enemy may relish seeing you fail, and instead will praise you dishonestly. Thus, be wary of any aspect that receives excessive praise; you may need to reconsider that part.

Rivals are valuable for evaluating your initiative, as they can highlight its potential weaknesses. If you are patient enough to tolerate their ongoing criticism, and smart enough to shield the system from their negativity, you can make the most of such critique. By tuning your awareness to their harsh feedback, and by gathering enough courage to face issues that others failed to raise, you do yourself and your initiative a favor.

In the first place, you send the system a clear sign that no issue is off the table; anything is open for discussion. This openness will affect the culture of your organization, limiting gossip and secret discussions. Moreover, once you filter your resisters' comments, you will be surprised by the number of valuable insights you end up with.

Keep in mind, however, that listening to what your opponents say does not necessarily mean validating their point of view. The eighth eye is just looking for data that can either keep you alive or help you thrive.

Keeping You in Check

Enemies give us a new perspective on reality. Take the news

channels. Our entire world (or more correctly, our interpretation of it) relies on the information they feed us. Focusing on one media platform and ignoring all the others will blind us to the other side of the story, and perhaps leave us unaware of a flaw in our worldview.

Those who support us are often biased and protective of us. They may be reluctant to slap us with harsh realities that may need to be heard. Our enemies, on the other hand, have no problem sharing their severe criticism. They tell us what we may need to hear. Thus, keeping an eye on them humbles us and keeps us grounded.

The eighth eye helps us accept criticism counterbalancing the excessively reassuring and optimistic feedback we might get from our supporters.

Yes, accepting criticism hurts, and yes, we are tempted to reject it. But what the opposition says to us is of great importance. When we learn to accept their feedback as a gift of awareness, we realize that what they are saying may prevent us from slipping into the trap of ego, which may seduce us into blindly following comments that are solely supportive.

Keeping our opponents on our radar also prevents us from declaring victory too soon. Announcing the triumph of a major leadership initiative as soon as the smallest success knocks at our door can be a terrible mistake. Too much reassurance can gradually fester into arrogance. Such an attitude will reduce our sense of urgency and may cause us to lower our guard. Not only does this attitude sap our momentum, it also opens the door for opposing forces to take over.

The eighth eye prevents us from indulging in our past triumphs. The data we gather from our competitors keeps us on our toes, bursting any victory bubble we might be enamored by. Even when our rivals signal that the struggle is over, our eighth eye keeps watching their intentions, monitoring their future moves for a potential comeback.

> **Keeping our eighth eye open prevents us from going overboard.**

Building Up Your Capital

Imagine this: You actually become friends with your competitors. Think of the impression you will leave on the system when you show empathy by getting to know your opposition and listening to their reality. For one thing, you won't seem as wicked as your rival's imagination may have painted you. Also, showing compassion usually lightens your opponent's aggression and curtails the efforts to block your way.

The energy your opposition will put into making your initiatives fail, could be channeled and redirected if you manage to gain their trust. You may be surprised to see some resisters even become supporters.

But before getting too close to the fire, it is important to make sure you're wearing the right gear. Unless you know how to agreeably differ in opinion, strategy, or values, getting too close can burn you.

Being compassionate with those who wish us harm and keeping them close can teach us many useful lessons, but it is very difficult to execute. It is important not to become paralyzed by the risks of keeping enemies at your doorstep; remember, not all your resisters can be turned into supporters.

Strengthening Your Shields

The eighth eye puts you on a fact-finding mission. Spending time with the opposition enables you to get to know them better, understand who they are, and how much pressure they feel in your presence.

Knowing your competitors helps you understand what the best course of action is in dealing with them. The same knowledge can help you choose suitable allies. Building an appropriate network of supporters will be impossible if you do not know what kind of opponents you have, how strong they are, and what they are planning to do.

By surrounding yourself with those who can and will add to your political capital, you will shield yourself from unexpected resistance by your enemies. Imagine that a competitor in the Human Resources (HR) department impedes your promotion. It would be smart to get to know that enemy and the people around him or her. Get to know the dynamics of the relationship between that person and the person's colleagues and superiors. Why not become allies with one of the superiors? Not in the spirit of harming the person, but in the spirit of surviving and growing within your company.

Keeping your eighth eye open gives you a better chance to build the alliances that will keep you alive. Alliance-building applies not only to the business world, but to your personal life as well. Think of a neighbor who makes your life seem like a never-ending wrestling competition: Who gets the best parking spot, who has the best Christmas decorations, etc. Getting to know his real intentions will help you understand the situation better. If he simply enjoys a little rivalry to feel alive, then so be it. If he really resents you and wants you out of the neighborhood, then it would be wise to think of preemptive moves (as in getting to know why he resents you, perhaps discussing your differences) so that you can start to live more harmoniously and not end up hating the neighborhood.

The more you know your opponents, the better you can plan to face them and neutralize or prevent their actions. Think of a football team getting ready for their final match in the championship. Now imagine that the two opposing teams were not allowed to know who their opponent would be until the teams took to the field. How different would their preparations and practice be? How much easier would it be for the team to prepare for their big event if they knew who they were up against? And how much easier would it be if one of their players was an ex-player from the opposing team? Knowing your opponent makes it so much easier to prepare for competition.

Why Is the Eighth Eye Important for Leadership?

As I mentioned before, thinking politically is at the heart of leadership work. When mobilizing your system, different groups will emerge on the political map of your organization or community. You will notice that not only will you have to manage your authority figures, but that an important part of your system is made up of those who do not like you personally or oppose your initiatives. Your enemies require as much management as your allies or bosses do.

Succeeding in your initiative may require you to work as closely with your opponents as you do with your supporters. Staying connected to the opposition is not an easy task, but is critical. Since one task of leadership is to make sure that growth continues, open communication is necessary. Every organization needs to create and nurture a business philosophy in which anyone has the right to an opinion and can voice it freely. The challengers to your initiative are among the key players who can help you polish it and lead the way to success, if you learn how to handle them.

The focus of your eighth eye should be on every possible opponent you may have, whether a vicious neighbor or a business competitor. The eighth eye's awareness will keep you one step ahead of your opponents and allow you to adapt your moves to keep the enemy off guard.

> *"If you know the enemy and know yourself, you need not fear the result of a hundred battles. If you know yourself but not the enemy, for every victory gained you will also suffer a defeat. If you know neither the enemy nor yourself, you will succumb in every battle."*
>
> - SUN TZU

The Enemy Within

"We have met the enemy and he is us"

- WALT KELLY

Lastly, it is important to note that sometimes your eighth eye will sadly tell you that your enemy — perhaps even your nemesis — looks you in the eye whenever you stare at the mirror. It is important that when thinking of the concept of an enemy, we don't limit the concept to the outside world, but also apply it to what happens on the inside.

Any thought or emotional disposition that stands in the way of your survival and growth is your enemy. This is where your first eye may lend a hand. The self-awareness that your first eye affords you will help you pinpoint what is standing in your way. It could be your fear of commitment, your self-consciousness, your lack of belief in yourself, or your lack of effort. There is only one way to handle these enemies, once identified. Just like with any other enemy, you must understand where these insecurities or obstacles stem from. Awareness is essential. From there, you will be able to exercise compassion and patience with yourself and take one step at a time to overcome these obstacles.

Whose eyes are these?

THE TEN EYES OF LEADERSHIP

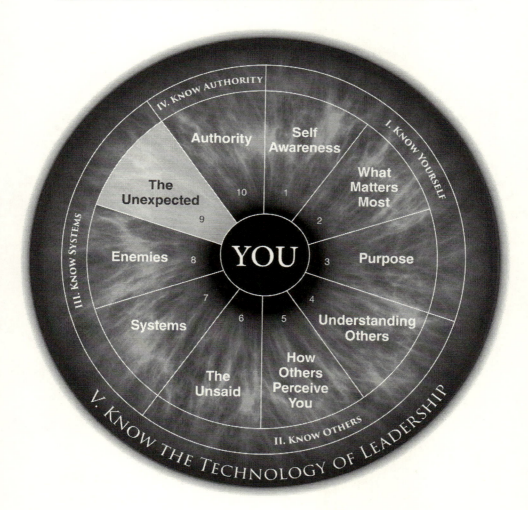

CHAPTER TEN

THE NINTH EYE: THE UNEXPECTED

Buckle Up and Brace Yourself

Life is filled with incidents and possibilities that can break our daily routine. Some of these so-called surprises are happy moments that give us joy, and some are heartbreaking.

We encounter several unexpected events every day, ranging from mild moments of "oh, okay" to ghastly "Oh my God" episodes. As the Greek philosopher Heraclitus once said, "Change is the only constant," because nothing in life stands still. If it did, there would be no progress. So how do we prepare ourselves?

We must realize that certainty is merely an illusion, for even if you planned out every step of your life, you can never know what the environment has in store for you. We fool ourselves by believing in certainty, and then we are dismayed when we realize that predictability is an unachievable fantasy. One of the major sources of emotional pain is the disappointment one feels when expectations are unmet or when one discovers that life is unstable. Change is a fact of life and we need to accept it.

Most of us like to be in control of our lives. Most of us find ourselves comfortable with mundane and predictable everyday life. This is normal. We feel safer in controllable and familiar surroundings, where we repeat the same actions each day, without surprises or spikes. Unexpected events take us out of our comfort zone, causing us stress and anxiety. But since life is dynamic and ever-changing, the role of your ninth eye is crucial. It is the eye on the unexpected, bringing us awareness of the possibility of changes that could unfold and preparing us to handle these changes without compromising our survival and growth.

Ready or Not, Here I Come

Who hasn't had to deal with an "Arrrgghh" moment? Unforeseen incidents are a normal part of the game, and they will strike whether we are ready or not. Since life is obviously unpredictable, it is up to us to either be crippled by its irregularity, or be ready to capitalize on what is thrown our way.

Think of these examples of unwelcome and unpredictable events. How often do they happen, if not to you, then to those around you?

- Your baby gets a high fever in the middle of the night.
- You get into a car accident.

- You get cheated on.
- A natural disaster (hurricane, earthquake, flood, and wildfire) strikes.
- You get mugged.
- Your business lands suddenly in the middle of a scandal — or you do.
- Your company suffers a sudden loss or the death of a key executive.
- An economic or political crisis takes place in your country.

As Julius Caesar said, "No one is so brave that he is not disturbed by something unexpected." We are doubly disturbed by events such as the previous examples, which are not only unexpected, but upsetting. However, accepting that some events are unpredictable and unavoidable is the first step to being able to deal with these ups and downs. Employing your ninth eye will make you better equipped to tackle life's surprises with confidence.

However monotonous your life might seem, there is always the probability of an unforeseen event lurking for you around the corner.

Panicking is NOT an Option

I was once driving home at night at a time when there is usually no traffic and was utterly shocked by the number of cars on the road barely moving. After a few loooong minutes, I left my car to see what was going on. As I approached, I realized that there had been a minor car accident. Two cars had barely scratched each other, and the worst damage was that the second car's front light was slightly broken. That's it.

But that was not what was holding up traffic; it was the driver of the second car, who was making a scene. He was hysterically running around on the highway screaming and shouting in total panic because of the impact and shock of the unexpected occurrence of the accident. He was making a big fuss about the whole incident, which in turn created more tension and fear in the people around him than the accident itself.

Had this man opened his ninth eye, he would have been prepared for such an incident; he would neither have panicked nor made a scene. When someone panics, especially an authority figure, everyone around him or her will panic and nothing good can come of it. Imagine a doctor having a panic attack while performing surgery. Can you picture the fear he will instill in all the other doctors and nursing staff?

When exercising leadership, you are under the spotlight. The tone of voice and attitude of the lead surgeon, during a time where the patient is at risk, determines whether the rest of the team will panic or not. His composure will determine that of the system. The same applies to pilots. If you have ever flown on a plane, the only true comfort you have during turbulence is the calm and composed expressions on the cabin crew's faces. Even the calm and collected announcement that the pilot makes to remain seated due to turbulence. If he were to come on the intercom and start to panic and say, "cabin crew stay seated" then heads would roll.

Another example further emphasizes this point. During a spacewalk by a Canadian astronaut outside the international space station, something went wrong with the astronaut's suit. Some kind of vapor seeped through, fogging up his mask and reducing his visibility to zero. Just imagine the situation: You have limited oxygen and you are hanging in, without any sense of direction or vision of where you are. Instead of panicking however, he kept in contact and eventually they were able to find a solution. His heart beat never exceeded 100 BPM. This shows that his ninth eye was extremely trained, as he realized the importance of not panicking, remaining clear-headed and looking for a quick and efficient solution. Imagine if he did panic, floating in space moving around abruptly, consuming energy and not coming up with a practical solution. It would have been his demise. In his case, it meant the difference between life, death, or getting trapped in space.

Panic is never an option, especially when exercising acts of leadership. The ninth eye will reinforce you with an internal shield, preparing you for the battles ahead, and it will give you resilience to cope with whatever comes your way. Panicking or avoidance will not solve anything; neither will feeling bad for someone else or sorry for yourself. These are all reactive reflexes. This is where the importance of your ninth eye lies. It allows you to be responsive rather than reactive, enabling you to move forward despite the unforeseen challenges.

The ninth eye prevents you from panicking. Panic is contagious and will take away from your credibility and stance within a system. It will be hard for you to mobilize others if you are not even in control of yourself.

Welcome to Our Flight Simulator (Role of the Ninth Eye)

The ninth eye introduces you to flight simulator training. A flight simulator creates an artificial aircraft flight along with the environment surrounding it. It is an essential part of pilot training, exposing pilot candidates to factors such as turbulence or an engine going down, so that they can be prepared for real-life flights. You don't have to be a pilot to get this type of training. All you need to do is to open your ninth eye and allow it to prepare you. And what better time to be prepped for turbulence than during times of stability and peace?

"It is a common defect in man not to make any provision in the calm against the tempest,"

- MACHIAVELLI

There's Often a Signal

Through the awareness that the ninth eye provides, you can start picking up on signals of a potential change; and yes, there usually are signals. There are not many real surprises in life. We just must train our ninth eye to pick up those signals and equip ourselves accordingly.

Let's take the following example of a family that lives in an area known for hurricanes. If the family has seen the damage and destruction that befalls anyone who encounters a hurricane, but doesn't take obvious precautions such as securing their house and buying safety equipment, their ninth eyes are sewn shut. Human weakness occurs when we think of ourselves as indestructible and believe "it would never happen to me." This line of thinking could prevent you from taking proper precautions, even when signs of danger are clear and evident. In the case of the family in hurricane-country, when the weather report comes out and it is too late to prepare, we can expect this family to panic.

> *"There is only one kind of shock worse than the totally unexpected: The expected for which one has refused to prepare."*
>
> - MARY RENAULT

Do you remember the rise and fall of the BlackBerry device? The bottom line was they didn't know the storm was coming. BlackBerry Limited (called Research in Motion, or RIM, at the time) was a tech giant, and its executives felt they were invincible. They had won the battle against Motorola and Palm. But their great decline came in 2007, when Apple introduced the iPhone. At first, BlackBerry Limited did not feel threatened, because top management was blind to the shifts in the market. Consumers wanted touch displays, better browsing options, dual cameras, and lots and lots of games and apps, but Blackberry clung to email.

Yes, it really did have the best and safest platform for wireless emailing, and it was working tirelessly on innovation when it came to top messaging services, email, and security. But the world was shifting, and BlackBerry lagged behind. Along with other giants, Apple, Samsung, and Google created new concepts for smartphones. BlackBerry ended up with two options: a sale or a joint venture. The unexpected hit and they weren't ready.

Refining Your Ninth Eye

We are blessed with sharp instincts, gut feelings, and quick reflexes that have kept us alive. Listening to that internal voice allows us to make quick but wise decisions when responding to unpredictable situations. When you are on alert and paying attention to the details, many occurrences are not that unexpected after all.

"There can be as much value in the blink of an eye as in months of rational analysis."

- MALCOLM GLADWELL

We can refine these responses and awareness further by developing our ninth eye and allowing it to function efficiently. This eye provides you with a thorough and analytical understanding of the data around you, and it helps you listen carefully, scrutinizing every piece of evidence that suggests future trouble. It prevents you from standardizing events to make them fit into what you consider normal. When something stands out, the ninth eye pushes you to examine it, instead of ignoring it.

So, to help this eye do its job, pay attention to details. Of course, you need to keep a balance, since it is possible to let details distract you from the big picture, and it is physically and mentally impossible to always be aware of everything all the time.

Taking the time to review your day regularly, whether early in the morning or late at night, will provide you with key insights on the signals you should recognize and deal with. Over time, as this daily contemplation becomes an entrenched habit, you will probably realize that your judgment about life's unexpected spikes has significantly improved.

Paying attention to how things are going on a daily basis allows your ninth eye to pick up patterns, and consequently irregularities, which could signal that something is off. Engaging in mindfulness and meditation is also an excellent way to gain wisdom and courage, and hence respond decisively to unexpected blows.

By keeping an eye on past hiccups in life, the ninth eye makes you stronger to face future obstacles. Your previous failures give you indications of weaknesses in your organization, family, or personal life, so you can strengthen those areas.

Some of the most significant lessons on handling the unexpected may arise from those who have ventured out before us. They have experienced similar events and lived through many of the incidents we might encounter. They are thus in the best position to help our ninth eye. If we have the courage and wisdom to listen to their guidance, they can broaden our horizons and suggest "just in case" alternatives. Of course, sometimes we have no other option but to experiment all alone and attempt to manage life's surprises as we move forward.

> *"Prepare for the unknown by studying how others in the past have coped with the unforeseeable and the unpredictable."*
>
> - GEORGE S. PATTON

The Beauty of the Calm Amid a Storm

The consciousness of your ninth eye injects you with tranquility and inner strength. The moment you acknowledge that anything can happen and tune your mind to adapt to any conflict, external events lose their power over you. The calmness and detachment you will experience will diffuse the agitation that results when a surprise interrupts your normal schedule. You will be blessed with indifference and equanimity, in spite of the fact that no matter how carefully you plan events, things that are out of your control will happen.

This calmness keeps us open to new experiences and learning, and allows us to move forward. If you always have a preferred condition in which you operate, and you fail to function in other conditions, you are placing limits on your survival and growth. Your ninth eye ensures that you are not stuck inside the borders of your comfort zone.

> *"Men are wise in proportion, not to their experience, but to their capacity for experience."*
>
> - GEORGE BERNARD SHAW

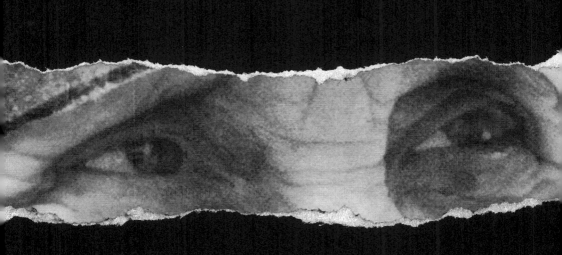

Whose eyes are these?

The Ninth Eye Keeps You Adaptive

Your ninth eye makes you more flexible and resilient. Just as water takes the shape of any container, your ninth eye helps you adapt to any new condition or problem you face. Adaptation is wired within us. Think of the times when you are in a lit room and then the lights suddenly go out. At first, you cannot see a thing. But your pupils start dilating and adapting to the darkness, soon enabling you to see figures and shadows. This adaptability also applies to any changes we might experience. Our bodies and emotions are made to accommodate and readjust, regardless of how much pain or time it may take. The awareness of the ninth eye makes this process faster and less painful.

It Is Not as Bad as You Think

Some people are inherently more optimistic than others, and manage to see a hidden blessing in every curve ball life throws at them. However, for those who are less optimistic, employing the ninth eye will help them take the hit more positively and see value in the change inflicted. Maybe it was a change of routine; it was a great lesson, it taught you a new skill, it was an opportunity in disguise, or it opened a window for something new and exciting in your life.

Unless we develop a more positive attitude toward life's surprises, we will not be able to properly handle them. This is not to suggest that every unwelcome intrusion is a sacred sign or a doorway to a fresh beginning. We all have experienced unexpected complications that left us shattered (the death of a loved one, the breakup of a relationship, the loss of a job we need). We cannot respond to such events like robots. It takes time to work through the pain of a major loss, and to come to the point where we can think more optimistically about our future. We need to be patient with ourselves at such times, and grief is often our most appropriate immediate response. But with the awareness that the ninth eye gives us, everything will have a more tolerable impact on us.

Ninth Eye Disclaimer

The ninth eye cannot guarantee that we will never make mistakes responding to surprises; it will, however, make us more confident about the choices we make. It increases our alertness to what we need to do.

The ninth eye is not about being pessimistic. On the contrary, awareness increases our optimism about life's unexpected events, especially those that seem to be setbacks. Keeping your ninth eye open does not necessarily mean avoiding risks or becoming crippled with fear by expecting the worst. The ninth eye is about being a realist and being prepared. The trick is to find the right balance between being overly optimistic (living in LaLa Land) and being too pessimistic (crippled by fear).

The ninth eye is not going to make you a fortune-teller. After all, if we knew the future, nothing would be pleasant or fascinating. Imagine knowing every ending to every movie you watch or every book you read. Imagine knowing how things are going to unfold every time you go out on a date. How different and mundane would life be? The role of your ninth eye is merely to prepare you for however life decides to treat you.

The ninth eye identifies unexpected circumstances that could happen, but that is not enough. It is then your job to discover the effects these events are likely to have on your survival and growth, so that you can be ready and prepare yourself accordingly.

Your ninth eye is not about becoming paranoid or worrying about every single detail that may creep up on you. It is simply about awareness. It is not about replaying tragic scenarios in your head. Repetitive fearful thoughts can build into an unbearable anxiety.

Practice Makes Perfect

The ninth eye helps you evaluate what can be done, if at all possible, to prevent the problem from occurring in the first place.

The alertness of your ninth eye will suggest that you practice your speech, prepare your presentation ahead of time, and keep extra provisions ready for any emergency. By expecting and rehearsing stressful situations before they occur, you give your mind the ability to focus on generating solutions instead of getting stuck in the mode of, "How did this happen?!"

Prevention and planning are always a safer bet than responding on the spot to a nerve-wracking incident.

Your "Just in Case" Portfolio

By going through the challenging scenarios you might encounter, you are already setting up your mind to prepare for the coming hurdles and scan for potential solutions. The more you train yourself to pick up signs from your environment and adjust accordingly, the more extensive your solutions kit is. This preparation increases your readiness for times when things do not go as planned. When all is going well, you will never need to flip through this list of solutions. But the moment you are taken by surprise, you will be glad it is there, offering you a way out.

Your ninth eye is focused on what can be done to deal with the things that you can change. It is not about dwelling on the things you cannot influence. Your ninth eye allows you to adjust to the circumstances you currently face, instead of getting trapped in nagging or wishful thinking.

It is essential to have a reliable backup and a solid Plan B, with all the support you can get. "Do not put all your eggs in one basket". Does this proverb sound familiar? That is your ninth eye talking. When activated, the ninth-eye awareness invites you to look at alternatives in the event your original plan fails. This vigilance prevents you from feeling powerless, anxious, and not knowing what to do next.

Forget About Control

What is in your control?

Take a few minutes to list what is actually within your scope of power. You will soon realize that, out of the countless things that come to your mind, very few actually are within your control. No one can confidently state, "I have ordered a clear sky for my party," or "I booked a flight without turbulence."

The ninth eye is not about controlling the unexpected, but about foreseeing what can go wrong. It is about imagining the right circumstances for success and the obstacles that might delay it. When you realize that you are fretting about silly stuff, ask yourself, "Is this helping me?" or, "Is this within my control?"

You will find that losing sleep is not the most productive way to handle the unexpected; your energy and time are better invested on something within your control.

The Messy World of Leadership

If life is messy, leadership work is messier. Leadership is about creating appropriate interventions to make life better, fix problems, create opportunities, change values, and readjust loyalties. What can be more unpredictable than a person, or an entire system, under the heat of leadership work?

Leadership is needed less during stable periods, and more during spikes and disturbances of the status quo. It is in these spikes that it is possible for the system to falter and move backward; hence leadership is required to make sure the spike does not become a setback and that the system continues to move forward. Leadership requires that we learn to thrive on interruptions and shifts, and to responsively handle them in a wise manner.

The feedback of your ninth eye doesn't come from just one source of knowledge, skills, or resources; it involves other people, other experts. When trouble strikes, it encourages you to recruit or hire the person or team with the most expertise and experience in the field to take charge and make decisions. Leadership in such times should not be based on rank and status.

The ninth eye prevents you from slipping into anxiety as a reaction to a sudden event. It allows you to turn any interruption into something fruitful instead of allowing it to damage your credibility within a system.

The alertness that the ninth eye instills in you helps you keep your composure and exude confidence, regardless of the situation you are in. This equanimity is vital to leadership roles.

How Do You Cope with the Unfamiliar?

Consider these questions, which the ninth eye can help you answer:

- When was the last time you were unsettled by a spike or interruption?

- What threatening signs have you discounted lately?
- In what areas do you need to stretch your scope of vision?
- How do you respond to the unexpected?
- What unexpected events caught your attention in the past month?
- Do you feel disappointed or angry because something unexpected happened?
- Do you panic or become stressed when something unexpected happens?
- In which areas of your life do you believe you will be devastated if something hits you?

While some may collapse under the weight of the unexpected, others will find ways to prosper and rise above the hard times. Fortunately, you can study and practice how to effectively manage life's unpredictability. Just as a doctor learns to deal with the pressure of potentially losing a patient's life, so you can learn to remain calm and alert when the need arises.

Consider the example of an unexpected power outage. When your work is suddenly interrupted by a power blip or technical failure, although you may not be able to send the emails or do normal work on your internal system, there are still tasks you can do while the power is out. You can still draft correspondence you've been planning to mail, sort out administrative stuff, or maybe catch up on reading that was piling up.

You can never fully expect the unexpected. But you can be prepared to strike it down and counterattack. The goal of the ninth eye is to, first of all, reduce, as much as possible, the repercussions of those events, then turn as many of the unexpected events into anticipated events so as to lose the surprise factor. Finally, you prepare yourself to react properly when the unexpected hits. In other words, be ready. The ninth eye is about having what it takes to keep moving forward, to stay alive and thrive.

> *"Embrace and expect every bump, twist, and curve in the road. Understand that it will always be there and accept it for what it is because it is a part of the rich beauty of your life. Meet every challenge with vigor knowing that you'll be a stronger and better person."*
>
> - J. CHAREST

Whose eyes are these?

PILLAR IV
KNOW AUTHORITY

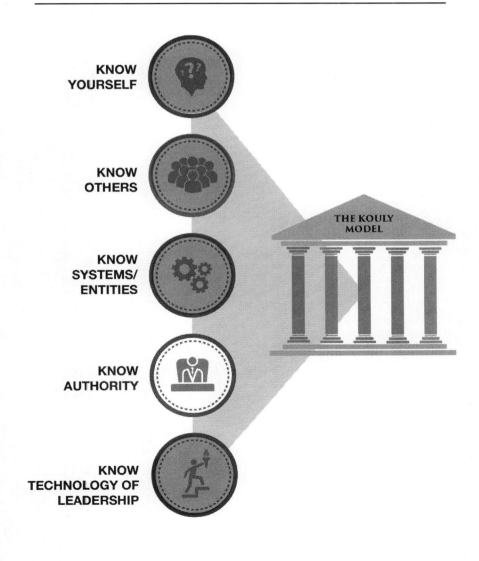

THE TEN EYES OF LEADERSHIP

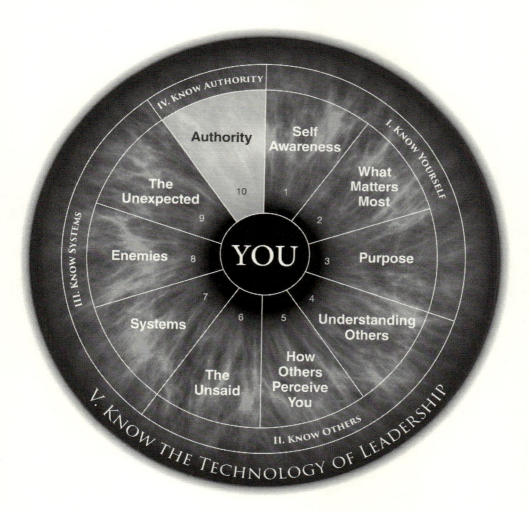

CHAPTER ELEVEN

THE TENTH EYE: AUTHORITY

I stumbled upon a story that may sound fictional but, unfortunately, it really happened!

After a long week of back-and-forth negotiations with one of their most important suppliers, the company's negotiating team managed to have the supplier agree to a twenty-five percent discount.

The negotiating team kept the news from their boss, as they wanted to surprise him with their success after signing the contract. And then it happened... just as they were about to seal the deal, their boss stormed into the meeting room, snatched the contract from the table, and started to tear it up. Then he looked at his negotiating team and said, "This deal took a week's time for four people! That means two hundred hours! Now, watch how things are supposed to be done."

He then stared at the supplier's sales manager and confidently said, "Fifteen percent off — yes or no?"

The room went so silent; you could have heard a pin drop.

When he saw the supplier's sales manager looking pleased and nodding silently, the boss turned to his negotiating team and said, as he was heading toward the door, "I hope that teaches you something."

And it did.

And That's How It's Done!

The relationship with authority requires delicacy and tact. I still wonder where the problem really started in this scenario. Was it when the boss's ego and excitability completely hijacked the negotiations? Or was it when his team remained silent, seemingly saving face, but costing the company a lot of money? Either way, one thing you must be aware of, and you will understand once you continue reading, is the need to keep authority informed. Had the employees kept their boss in the loop, neither he nor they would have looked like fools.

Both parties should be held responsible for the events that transpired that day, but similar problems are sure to happen when people do not invest the time or effort to understand authority and learn how to work with authority. Dealing with authority is as critical for our survival and growth as being aware of ourselves (first eye) and understanding how the system works (seventh eye). The following pages will help you activate the tenth eye, an eye that is dedicated to authority.

This new awareness will:

- **Keep you alive.** You will discover how not understanding authority can drain your resources and slow down or limit your advancement personally, corporately, socially and financially — and that's the minimum penalty. At worst, not understanding authority can kill you.

- **Help you prosper.** A good relationship with authority will positively influence your growth.

- **Improve your leadership skills.** Just think how many initiatives have been cut short because people did not put enough effort into getting authority on board.

Why Should You Even Care?

From the moment you are born and for as long as you choose to remain a part of society (unless you are a hermit in some lost mountain), you will always be interacting with figures of authority in many forms. Authority can be an individual (such as a father, a head of a department, a police officer, a restaurant owner, an expert on a subject, a boss, or even a president). Authority can also be a group (such as a board of directors), an institution (such as a parliament or the United Nations), or even a country. Authority can also be a moral figure or an abstract spiritual concept (such as God).

Thus, even if you had the privilege of living alone, being self-employed and not reporting to anyone, it would still be impossible for you to shield yourself completely from authority. Authority figures have power over you, and the way authority sees you shapes your life. Your manager could lay you off, your football coach could pin you on the bench for the entire season, and your biology professor could give you a failing grade. When a police officer asks you to park your car and show your identification papers, you will listen whether you like it or not, unless you want to spend the night in jail. But having a good relationship with authority is not just about surviving; it can also help you prosper and lead others, for it gives you access to their resources that are exclusive to them and their wisdom.

> **No matter its form, dealing with authority is a fact of life simply because no system exists without authority.**

It is Not as Bad as You Think

For many, the word "authority" conveys a negative meaning and is associated with equally intimidating terms such as power, control, abuse, dominance, and manipulation. The term is frequently associated with being bossy, abusive or overbearing, so that many are highly skeptical of authority and choose to dismiss it altogether. And they may be right. All too often, authority has been misused. However, our problems with authority stem from the intentions of those in power and the way they exercise their authority, rather than with the concept of authority itself.

Like many other species, humans were born and evolved as part of systems, enjoying the protection and cooperation offered by the group. Systems soon discovered their survival was maximized by appointing a coordinator, or authority figure, solely dedicated to providing the group with what it needs to survive and thrive: guidance, food on the table, protection from outside danger, as well as law and order within the group. And this is how authority emerged.

The purpose of authority in groups is to secure the group's existence by ensuring a constant and steady provision of the services needed for the group's survival and growth.

Take a few minutes to apply this to your own figures of authority. What benefits would you expect from your parent as your authority figure? Your boss? Your government? God?

Without authority, humankind would not have the basic support for its survival and growth.

An Uneven World

If authority is just a simple coordinator the system selects to serve its needs and deliver clear direction, then why do things seem more complicated?

Well, so that those coordinators can fulfill their responsibilities, the group endows them with **power** and **resources** to facilitate their performance and effectiveness. Power and resources could include money, manpower (hiring and firing), access to information, privileges, the right to use violence and other corrective mechanisms, veto rule, decision-making abilities, power of signature, etc.

For example, in most countries, the system has authorized the president to make decisions on its behalf regarding survival and growth matters related to the country (such matters as economy, defense, external policy, internal security). Similarly, a CFO has been given power to make finance-related decisions within the company for a given period.

> **The concept of authority is a trade between the system and the authority figure, where power and trust are granted in exchange for services.**

The Down Side of Power

The exchange of power between authority and the system is a simple transactional relationship: As long as the authority is performing its role, the contract is renewed. **When authority fails to perform its role:**

1. The contract is either suspended and authority replaced (using peaceful or democratic means, or in some cases more extreme methods), or

2. If replacement is not possible, the system waits until a more suitable option emerges.

Most authority is therefore naturally vigilant and defensive about its status and the privileges it can access. Many authority figures will go to great lengths to sustain their role, and are paranoid or perhaps even obsessed with what they can do to stay in power and expand it.

This is not to imply that authority is a bad thing. On the contrary, authority is a good thing, and in many instances, bad authority often proved to be far better than no authority.

No system in history has lasted long without an authority figure; any period between authority figures is usually a state of chaos. Just like any tool, authority's power can be devoted to good or bad purposes. When the people at the top forget that the privileges they receive are conditioned upon the services they provide the system, they can easily slip into the trap of abusing their power.

> *"Power tends to corrupt, and absolute power corrupts absolutely."*
>
> - LORD JOHN DALBERG-ACTON

You Versus Authority

Ever wondered why it is so daunting to address a person in authority?

Why do some of us look like a petrified rabbit when talking to the CEO, while others can angrily slam the door following an argument with their CEO?

How many people do you know who hop from job to job because they simply can't deal with any person in charge? Conversely, how many of your colleagues are excessive in their admiration for authority figures and spend all their efforts and energy to please them?

Why do some of us find it very difficult to set and keep boundaries with authority without feeling guilty? Such individuals end up carrying their burden alone, working lengthy shifts and silently accepting abusive remarks.

Why are there such different default behaviors toward those who hold power? How can we explain what we feel?

Dealing with our emotions toward authority figures can be tricky. We often find ourselves acting in inappropriate ways around them, only to realize at a much later stage in our lives that our problems were in fact not unusual.

Have You Really Left Home?

Laura was a great kid at heart, but her spoiled nature got the best of her throughout her entire life. She was the youngest child in a very rich family. Her parents were highly successful, yet they were not really involved in her life. Whenever a problem arose, they would fix it with money. She got her way all the time, and never had to take "No" for an answer.

Not surprisingly, this background manifested itself in Laura's self-discipline across various settings. At school, she was every teacher's nightmare. She shoplifted, missed college classes, and had to repeat several courses. When she was eventually exposed to the work environment, no one was shocked that she couldn't keep a job for more than a few months. She was good enough at the job, but with her attitude, she couldn't get along with co-workers. She gave freelancing a shot, thinking that way she could be her own boss. Yet again, the endeavor did not work. How could it work, when she failed to deliver her projects to the clients on time, always missing the deadline by weeks?

Our relationship with authority started a long time ago with our parents or guardians. We relied on them for survival and growth, while struggling to assert ourselves and manage the tricky dynamics of the relationship. This very first interaction with authority has a deep and broad influence on the way we perceive and handle subsequent authority figures. It is during this sensitive period that our default behaviors toward authority were created and cemented.

> **Our reactions and underlying feelings toward authority are primarily governed by the memories of our early exchanges with our first caretakers.**

Unfortunately, because very few of us had fully functional relationships with our caretakers, our relationship with authority is naturally tense. It is therefore a fact of human nature to fear, be intimidated by, be angry with, or be otherwise triggered by authority. However, given the weight that relationships with authority have on our life, it is important to understand the nature and intensity of the feelings we personally hold toward authority, and find ways to come to terms with them.

Recognizing Our Scars

"The first time I saw him, I knew this is going to be a bumpy ride. I don't know how to explain it, but something about him reminded me of my dad. His posture, his look, his tone of voice… Something I could not identify. The moment he called me in, I broke out in a cold sweat. He calmly greeted me while staring at my black flats. Then in a serious voice asked that I wear heels the next day. In my mind, it was my first day at work, and I found a way to mess it up with the chairman. I remember stuttering a few words, feeling very self-conscious. I tried to mumble an apology but my words got stuck in my throat. Then I burst into tears in his office." — From a participant in one of my executive leadership programs.

The baggage we have from our past with our parents or guardians will unfortunately be repeated in patterns with every other authority we come to meet, whether it is a teacher, a CEO, Board of Directors, or just the lifeguard at the swimming pool. (Note that for the purposes of this book, when talking about fixing your relationship with authority, I am referring to people, not institutions, spiritual figures, etc.)

Depending on the effects and potential scars we have carried with us from a young age, we will have a tendency either to rebel or to conform to authority figures later in life. Our default reactions to authority can stretch from absolute fear and blind respect (conforming to and pleasing authority) to total anarchy (rebelling against and challenging authority). Wherever we land on this spectrum (except for the lucky few who manage to be in the healthy middle), our relationship with authority will always be loaded with emotions.

We each form unique survival strategies in response to authority figures. Some may have learned that it is more appropriate to act docile or seemingly obedient, while others resort to impressing authority. Still others decide to dismiss authority altogether. Whatever our particular responses to authority, they are a pattern we have developed to protect ourselves and stay alive.

Not only are our scars from early experiences manifested in the way we deal with those in charge, they are also revealed in the way we exercise our own authority. Consider the way you deal with your staff, students, subordinates or kids, looking at your professional, social and personal life:

- Do you recognize any clashes or patterns with authority that have been silently lurking in the background? Maybe an argument with a police officer? Or a heated dispute with your math teacher? Or a conflict with the board of directors?
- What does this behavior tell you about the scars you carry?

The scars inflicted by our first authorities are carried with us into our everyday lives, including into our social, and more importantly, professional settings. A seemingly inoffensive remark by our manager can bring us to tears or fuel a glare of hatred in our eyes. This awareness is critical if we are to realize why some dynamics in our workplace or other settings are particularly inflammatory to some, yet seem mundane to others.

Once we become conscious of our scars from our primary authority figures, we are able to better understand the nature and intensity of our reactions to the current figures of authority in our life.

Activating Our Awareness of Authority

Staying alive and thriving in any system requires that we not only understand what our personal defaults with authority are, but also that we have the awareness and flexibility to adapt our innate reaction to meet our need to work with authority enough to stay alive. A harmonious relationship further requires that we understand what the defaults and expectations of the system's authority are. We need to recognize that any lack of compatibility between our reaction and the reaction from authority will be painful, mainly to ourselves. Finally, we must learn to negotiate with authority, to improve our chances of survival and growth.

Working with authority is surely easier said than done, but failing to do so is a certain route to major problems.

While taking an active approach to managing our relationship with authority is a challenging task, perhaps the first and foremost step is activating our tenth eye.

> **Those who dismiss authority or are blind to the impact it can have on their lives are in great danger. Would you take your eyes off a tiger that is glaring at you?**

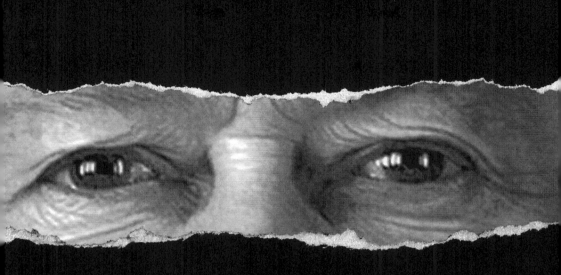

Whose eyes are these?

Big Brother is Watching

The moment you set foot in your parents' house or a hotel, on the street, or into your office, your privacy bubble is somehow invaded. Whether it is a parent, a hotel manager, the government, or your line manager, authority is always watching.

Take your CEO for example. Your CEO has his or her eyes on you 24/7, and for a legitimate reason. Monitoring what you do is part of what your CEO gets paid to do. Not only that, but your success or failure is tightly linked to that of your CEO's. The next time you fail to deliver on the assignments your CEO gave you, remember that you are putting your CEO in the line of fire.

While he or she may not always be present to personally observe you, your boss has one thousand and one ways to keep you on the radar. It is the job of bosses to find out what they need to know about you, from how early you get to the office, to how late you stay and how you handle conflict.

Why? Because no one can maintain a position at the top without being extremely alert. The risks at the top are too big to take lightly. This explains why authority, particularly a CEO, hates surprises, whether good or bad. The stakes are simply too high.

Authority desires to stay in power and expand its power. From this perspective, authority figures look at people as assets or liabilities, as supporters, threats, or even enemies. For authority, we are resources that help or hinder the progression of the system.

In this game, **nothing** is personal.

You are an asset to authority figures when:

1. You help them succeed (when you are professional).

2. You are loyal to them (when they trust you).

On the other hand, you become a liability to authority either by:

1. Becoming a threat (too rebellious, high-maintenance).

2. Not performing (not delivering on your tasks, not complying with authority's requests).

How much attention authority pays to you, whether it is your boss or a police officer, will hinge on how well you understand the authority and whether you meet the expectations authority figures have of you. Learning to handle their worries and calm their insecurities is the key to staying in the game, and hopefully winning their support.

Authority is constantly watching.

You are a resource among the many resources they have. It all boils down to this: Are you helping them deliver (meet the needs of the system and help them stay in power)?

There's no magical formula for building healthy relationships with authority, but awareness, loyalty, and professionalism are strong building blocks.

Through the awareness of the tenth eye, always ask yourself:

- In which areas am I being disloyal? In which circumstances am I a threat (emotional, physical, etc.) to authority's presence?

- In which areas am I not being professional (not delivering on my commitments, not reliable, not compliant)?

The Survival of the Fittest

How many competent employees get fired over trivial issues because they missed signals from their bosses? Similarly, how many not-so-particularly-talented co-workers got promoted because they knew how to make their boss recognize their accomplishments? This question does not apply only to your workplace. How many people are now in jail because they pushed authority too far too often?

> **Your ability to fit into a system without clashing with its authority is at least as crucial to your survival as being well-perceived by the system itself.**

It is naïve to believe that your promotions and success at work only depend on your hard work or intellectual abilities. Your competence and values are important but, sadly, are not enough. Being a pleasant and hardworking colleague will get you nowhere if you manage to get into daily arguments with your boss. Even if you don't argue with your boss, but stop being as valuable to him or her as you once were, you will likely be passed up for any promotion. It is important not only to be present, but also to be seen by those in charge.

Learning to be political with your authority figure is as critical as being smart, talented, and hardworking.

By learning to gauge your authority figure's reactions and make adjustments, you will be able to tell whether your employer sees you as high-maintenance or as a professional and key player.

The Tenth Eye in the Workplace

The tenth eye helps you gain insights into your boss, chairperson, or CEO's management style by observing his or her patterns and reactions. It helps you get to know him/her better: His or her preferred method of getting work done, the things he or she absolutely cannot stand, and how frequently your boss wishes to be informed. Once you understand your boss's psychology and approach to work, you will have a better understanding of what they value and a richer and more accurate reading of his or her mood. This understanding will allow you to adjust your actions to match their expectations and help in communicating ideas.

By understanding cues and signals from your boss, you will fulfill the tasks assigned to you more easily. The more your boss becomes clear and easy for you to read, the easier your job will become.

Keeping an eye on those in authority also allows you to anticipate their requests and meet their expectations ahead of time. When it comes to assignments and projects, your tenth eye reshuffles your everyday tasks to meet your boss's set of priorities. This prioritization includes being alert to sudden changes in the plan and accommodating last-minute requests. The last thing you want is to spend energy and time on tasks that are not in line with what your boss finds important.

> **Your tenth eye sees clearly that your priorities are your authority's priorities.**

When you concentrate on making the best of your relationship with your CEO, you become more attuned to your CEO's areas of weakness and the challenges he or she seems to get stuck in. With the help of your tenth eye, you will gradually know where your help is needed the most. By doing so, you will be increasing your bosses' (CEO or chairperson) dependence on you, supporting his or her success and guaranteeing yours.

Regulating the Tension

Conflict is bound to arise between you and authority. During heated discussions, the tenth eye allows you to pick up authority's signs of anger or tension and defuse them. Your awareness of authorities' responses prevents you from turning a cat into a tiger.

Keep in mind that the influence of authority comes from its ability to project power.

During the Middle Ages, punishment was imposed on the condemned in public squares, where everybody could watch and learn by example not to tamper with authority. Authority back then chose to display its power in public to remind the people of that power, because the minute authority appears vulnerable, it loses its influence over the people.

With your tenth eye fully focused on observing your authority's responses, you will be able to read the signals from his or her facial reactions and body language, knowing whether he or she approves of a subject. You will also know the right times to approach sensitive topics, such as asking for a raise or perhaps a long leave of absence or getting out of that long-standing parking ticket. The tenth eye will give you an idea of your authority's main concerns and will allow you to regulate your actions accordingly.

Do Not Mess with the Tiger!

I still recall this story from my school days. It was probably one of my earliest lessons on authority.

I had a strict and demanding math teacher in middle school. He was a tough character and hard to please. For some reason however, he seemed to be very harsh on all the students except me. He was always just a little bit easier on me than the rest of the students. One day, the class decided to file a complaint against his strict policies at the principal's office. The activist in me jumped in, eager to be among the first people to protest. As we were heading toward the office, I noticed that the group behind me started getting smaller and smaller. Students were changing their minds or chickening out. When I knocked on the principal's door, I discovered that I was all alone. I certainly didn't want to back out and look weak, so I boldly went in and filed a complaint. The teacher was then notified of my "personal" complaint and was mildly reprimanded.

From that day on, his classes became a nightmare. I do not recall a day when he did not pick on me or ask me to solve the toughest exercises on the board. I learned a hard lesson from seeing the students who had suggested that we report him sitting at their desks and laughing whenever he scolded me in front of the class.

And yes… I failed the class, for obvious reasons.

Authority is not perfect; but if you consider their point of view, authority figures are often trying their best to juggle their various responsibilities the best way they know how. Even if your authority is really at fault, the next time you feel the urge to publicly blame and criticize your authority, bring in the insights of your tenth eye to assess whether your move is strategic or doomed to blow up in your face. There is a very good chance that whatever you say about them will get back to them one way or another. The last thing you want is to be perceived as disloyal. Your lack of awareness of authority's potential retribution may cost you not only access to resources you could have had from the authority; in some cases, it could cost your life.

> *"Never strike a king unless you are sure you shall kill him."*
>
> - RALPH WALDO EMERSON

Are You Willing to Pay the Price?

Not keeping an eye on your authority has a deep impact on your survival and growth. Consider the following results:

- The ensuing unstable relationship between you and your authority will affect your health. Remember what happens after a bad fight with your boss or a parental figure to your stress level, blood pressure, sleep, and the long list of unhealthy habits such as smoking or overeating.

- Because the relationship with authority is deeply rooted in our system, any personal tension will likely spread to other relationships. How many times has a dispute with your boss affected your relationships outside the office?

- On a professional level, not managing your relationship with authority can stand in the way of your career advancement or even leave you unemployed. On a larger scale, the same bad relationship with authority can get you imprisoned, deported, or assassinated.

- The stress that such a fight creates leaves you drained and exhausted, which will slow your personal development and keep you busy with energy-draining trivial matters.

- Authority's paybacks can be ruthless, affecting your self-esteem or reputation at the very least. Such paybacks can reach the point of threatening your entire family.

- Being on authority's blacklist denies you any access to the authority's resources, and not only the financial resources. Think of all the connections, privileges, and information you could miss out on.

A Few Warnings

The data of the tenth eye is meant to help you deal with authority in an assertive and tactful way. In no instance should your awareness of authority's signals trap you in cycles of fear or abuse. The tenth eye's data should never restrict your opinion or turn you into a yes-man. On the contrary, the purpose of this awareness is to keep you alive and improve your prospects for growth. Thus, when necessary, the tenth eye will also make you aware when authority is taking you for granted and will suggest that you take corrective measures.

The tenth eye is like a radar antenna constantly scanning where you stand in your relationship with authority. Is your CEO ignoring you? Taking you seriously? Threatened by you? Why isn't your CEO maintaining eye contact? Why didn't your CEO address you during the entire meeting? Does your CEO seem engaged when you talk?

The tenth eye warns you when you have been below your authority's radar for more than a week. It warns you that your boss has absolutely no clue about the last deal you signed. It suggests that you therefore over-communicate in the coming period and keep your boss informed and reassured. Through the tenth-eye awareness, you will be able to weigh your boss's reactions to you and learn to negotiate the price of your loyalty.

The focus of the tenth eye should not only be on assessing how distant or upset your authority is, but also should pick up on the instances where your authority figure is highly responsive or very satisfied with your results. Being aware of these peak moments allows you to capitalize on them, asking for your deadline extension or budget raises.

The tenth eye also signals when authority seems closer than it should be. It allows you to keep the balance needed in your relationship. Failing to pick up these signals, and falling into the trap of becoming friends with your boss or teacher (even if he initiates this friendship), will not end well. When you become too close to him/her, you risk being accused of being favored, or of being a bootlicker trying to climb to the top. Besides, as a friend of the boss, it will be harder for you to draw a line between personal and professional life. Try turning him down the next time he invites you to a poker game at his house. (Didn't you promise your kids to take them to the movies that night?)

Keep it formal and friendly, never casual.

A Pot of Gold to Tap Into

When you have mastered your relationship with authority, the benefits are immeasurable. For example:

- The more you pay attention to those in authority, the more you get to know them and the greater your ability to empathize and work with them. Compassion and thoughtfulness can do wonders to enhance your relationship. The attention you receive and the bond you create will make your working environment smoother and more pleasant.

- Keeping your tenth eye open will help you build a solid and strategic relationship with authority. When your bosses become assured of your loyalty, they will support your efforts, fight battles for you, and defuse any potential opposition. Not only that, they are also likely to promote your cause with higher authorities. You will climb the ladder with them.

- Being on good terms with top executives will give you access to their pool of data and resources, which could be of immense help in that project you are championing.

- Not only do they have a comprehensive view of business matters from their higher position, they also are connected to a large group of constituencies. This access to connections and information will open up countless opportunities for your professional advancement.

- A good relationship with authority can also benefit your professional growth by giving you access to their know-how and expertise. Often authority didn't get to the top by accident. Being allowed to be close to the inner circle and exposed to their working style can teach you a lot about how to act, think, and respond in a similar working environment.

Time for a Checkup!

No matter how well you and your boss get along, taking your relationship for granted can put you in a precarious position. Unless you take the time to monitor the flow of your interaction and regularly assess both its strengths and weaknesses, difficulties in the relationship will gradually pile up. **The tenth eye invites you to take an objective look at your relationship with your own authority, with questions such as:**

- On a scale of one to ten, how well am I managing my relationship with my authority?
- How well do I get along with my direct figures of authority? Do I feel there are any pending unresolved issues between us?
- Do we trust each other?
- Do I understand my manager's expectations of me?
- Is my boss aware of what I need to meet his or her expectations? Is what I am doing making it easier for me to access his or her resources?
- Am I keeping my word and delivering? Am I acting in a professional manner?
- Am I loyal? Or am I perceived as a threat?
- Are there any red flags?
- What are the areas that I should pay attention to?
- Are they taking my loyalty for granted?

- On a scale of one to ten, how tense are my feelings toward authority?

- Are my feelings toward them positive? Negative? Indifferent?

- Where do these feelings stem from?

- What is this attitude toward authority costing me?

- What are the signs that my manager is sending me? Is he or she aware of the tasks I have completed and my accomplishments?

- Do I defend my boss when I talk to others about him or her and execute his or her goals?

- What could I do to support my manager more effectively?

Is Your Authority on Your Side?

Learning to manage authority is not only a matter of survival and growth, but of leadership as well. While you can certainly exercise leadership with or without authority, the success of any leadership initiative hinges on your ability to have authority on your side. Leadership is not just about challenging the system, but allowing it to move forward once it is going in the right direction. Leadership is about making the course of progression smoother.

It is already a risky endeavor to handle the complexities of any business or community which is reacting to the changes caused by your leadership. Facing the system's resistance without the backup of authority figures will certainly kill your initiative.

Similarly, implementing your plan without considering whose buy-in is critical to your initiative's success, would be a foolish waste of time, and is a sure way to put authority on the defensive. Your boss and other senior authority figures are the first people you need to have on board with your plan. Without their support, it will be almost impossible to move your ideas or projects forward.

Unless you brief authority figures thoroughly about your initiative, calm their potential fears and reassure them that your plan holds no risk to their standing and position, it will be almost impossible to see your project come to life. In fact, anything short of this comprehensive explanation will put you on their blacklist.

The tenth eye allows you to recognize the concerns of the authority figure regarding your project. It helps you identify the loyalties, fears, and resistance of a boss. Carefully observing your authority figures gives you indications about their current positions, their preferred outcomes, and the depth of their involvement, as well as their levels of power and alliances.

> **Exercising leadership requires negotiating with authority figures, either to have them on your side, or at least to guarantee they will not oppose your initiative.**

Whose eyes are these?

PILLAR V
KNOW TECHNOLOGY OF LEADERSHIP

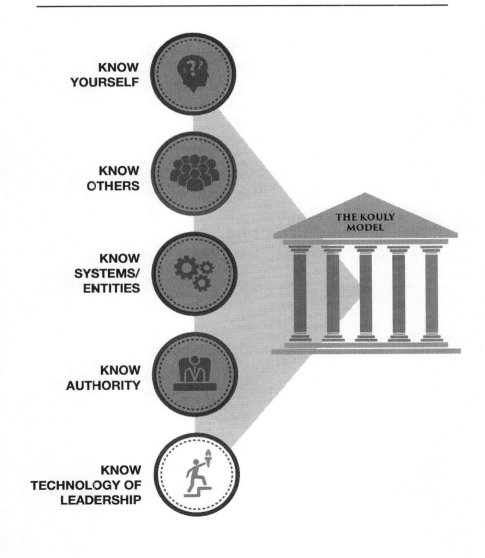

CHAPTER TWELVE

THE TECHNOLOGY OF LEADERSHIP

The technology of leadership or leadership engineering includes the tools, processes, gymnastics, aerobics, and techniques needed in the art of exercising leadership. Properly exercising leadership is a two-fold process:

The first requirement is about awareness; this is what the previous pillars build upon. The awareness of the self, others, systems, and authority. Once this knowledge has been accumulated, it aids in implementing the skills needed to place leadership in action.

The second requirement — this pillar — is all about the skills needed to implement the newfound awareness that you received from the 10 eyes. These skills include: Communication, negotiation, persuasion skills, body language, building alliances, team building, etc... All of which are subjects that become strengthened when using the awareness of the ten eyes. Nonetheless, these skills will not be delved into for the purposes of this book, as there are many very well-written books that tackle each of these subjects.

But it is important to note that all the four pillars above require the proper skills to translate what has been learned into concrete action. If you have all ten eyes open and yet have no knowledge about the art of communication or persuasion, then it will be difficult to truly exercise leadership. At the same time, if you have negotiation skills but have no proper awareness in differentiating the needs of others, this will also pose a threat and leave your attempts empty at best.

Awareness and skills go hand in hand. The awareness is the base, where the skills are used to refine the awareness and employ tools to get the most out of having your eyes wide open. Both come together and are needed. This book was written because most books focus on just the skills without giving readers the base or the awareness provided by the ten eyes. Hence, this book serves to bridge the gap and provide that information. We strongly recommend before you start exercising leadership that you focus both on awareness and refining your awareness through soft skills and techniques.

Whose eyes are these?

CHAPTER THIRTEEN

KEEP YOUR EYES WIDE OPEN

It is time to put things in motion. As you probably imagined, this step is a lot harder than you would like to think. This book is just the first step, awareness. What you choose to do with this information, how you use it from here on in, is up to you.

It is not enough to see the world with just your two physical eyes, because, as we know, our own two eyes can deceive us. We are not alone in this world; it is built upon systems and people, each following their own rules and regulations. Adaptation and understanding are essential to progress. But how will you adapt or understand if you are unaware of what is going on inside you, or even around you? How do you expect to lead yourself and others if you do not understand the systems that influence you?

Remember: Your first eye keeps your own thoughts, feelings, words and actions in check. How do you expect to understand others if you do not understand yourself? The second eye helps you focus on what matters the most. For some it is family, for others it is their career, and for some it is devoting themselves to their community. The third eye allows you to focus on what you love to do and share it with the world. The fourth eye lets you understand those around you, in order to help your fifth eye provide information on how others perceive you. Your sixth eye reads between the lines to make you aware of hidden intentions and the unsaid. Your seventh eye allows you to understand why the system reacts to you as it does. Your eighth eye examines your enemies' actions, schemes and plots. The ninth eye prepares you for the unexpected, for life, which sooner or later throws you curve balls. It is how you deal with the unexpected that makes the difference. The tenth eye makes you aware of how you deal with authority and how authority can affect your daily life and leadership abilities.

Do not forget that leadership originated to support the ultimate purpose of survival and growth. These days with the constant distractions we are in need of acts of leadership in our own lives, professionally and personally. To be an effective leader takes much more than the skills and techniques popularly associated with leadership. You need the awareness that comes from knowing yourself, others, systems and authority. You need to open your Ten Eyes of Leadership. Why? Because you must not allow your own insecurities and thoughts to stand in the way of what is good for the system or what needs to be done. Because you need to be aware of your environment, how the system is reacting to your interventions, where you will meet the most resistance (your enemies), and who you will need on your side (authority). Because, when you are focused on what really matters and have a purpose that will unite and direct everyone, the Ten Eyes of Leadership will allow you to excel in your leadership.

Reminder: Although it is one's personal responsibility to develop and sharpen these eyes, it is important to recognize that no one will have perfect vision of the ten eyes. Therefore, it is a necessary and smart strategy to create your supporting network of trusted individuals who may play the various roles of these eyes in your life. People like family, friends, colleagues and allies who could provide you with data about the reality of the environment surrounding you. You may even reciprocate and consider doing the members of your support structure a favor by playing some of the roles of these ten eyes in their lives. This way you may help them become more aware of their surroundings, offering them feedback and data to help their survival and growth.

Open your eyes, not just the ones you use for sight, but the ones you really SEE with. Are you happy with what you see?

NOTES

Introduction

1. Burton, James. "The 25 safest countries in the world." *WorldAtlas*, 23 Dec. 2015, www.worldatlas.com/articles/safest-countries-in-the-world.html.

2. Heifetz, Ronald A., and Marty Linsky. *Leadership on the line staying alive through the dangers of leading.* Harvard Business Review Press, 2002.

3. Heifetz, Ronald A. *Leadership without easy answers.* Belknap Press, 2003.

4. Heifetz, Ronald Abadian, et al. *The practice of adaptive leadership: tools and tactics for changing your organization and the world.* Harvard Business Press, 2009.

5. June, Dwuan. "World suicide rates by country." *The Washington Post*, www.washingtonpost.com/wp-srv/world/suiciderate.html.

6. Williams, Dean. *Real leadership: helping people and organizations face their toughest challenges.* Berrett-Koehler, 2005.

7. "Universal declaration of human rights." *United Nations*, United Nations, www.un.org/en/universal-declaration-human-rights/index.html

Chapter 1

1. "Five reasons why Macron won the French election." *BBC News*, BBC, 7 May 2017, www.bbc.com/news/world-europe-39791036.

2. Heifetz, Ronald A. *Leadership without easy answers*. Belknap Press, 2003.

3. Heifetz, Ronald A., and Marty Linsky. *Leadership on the line staying alive through the dangers of leading*. Harvard Business Review Press, 2002.

4. "Jamil Mahaud: 1949-: Political Leader Biography." *Mahuad, Ecuador, Government, and Public - JRank Articles*, biography.jrank.org/pages/3398/Mahaud-Jamil-1949-Political-Leader.html.Branford, Becky.

5. Kassin, Saul, et al. *Social psychology*. 9th ed., Cengage Learning, 2013.

Chapter 2

1. Beck, Judith S. *Cognitive therapy: basics and beyond*. Guilford Press, 2011.

2. Bradberry, Travis, and Jean Greaves. *Emotional intelligence 2.0: the world's most popular emotional intelligence test*. TalentSmart, 2009.

3. Gordon, Evian. *Brain revolution: know and train new brain habits*. Dog Ear Publishing, 2016.

4. Haidt, Jonathan. The happiness hypothesis: finding modern truth in ancient wisdom. Basic Books, 2006.

5. Kahneman, Daniel. *Thinking, fast and slow*. Farrar, Straus and Giroux, 2015.

6. Morris, Desmond. *The naked ape: the controversial classic of man's origins*. Dell Publishing, 1967.

7. Ruiz, Don Miguel. *The four agreements*. Center Point Publishing, 2008.

8. Schwartz, Jeffrey, and Rebecca Gladding. *You are not your brain: the 4-step solution for changing bad habits, ending unhealthy thinking, and taking control of your life*. The Penguin Group, 2011.

9. Shenk, David. *The genius in all of us.* Anchor Books, 2010.

10. "The chemical composition of tears varies depending on why we cry." *Discovery-Zone*, 18 Oct. 2013, www.discovery-zone.com/chemical-composition-tears-varies-depending-cry/.

Chapter 3

1. Steiner, Susie . "Top five regrets of the dying." *The Guardian*, 1 Feb. 2012, www.theguardian.com/lifeandstyle/2012/feb/01/top-five-regrets-of-the-dying.

Chapter 4

1. Celestine, Avinash. "Love's labour brings down hill." *The Indian Express*, 24 May 1997, archive.indianexpress.com/Storyold/1981/.

2. Chopra, Deepak. *The seven spiritual laws of success: a practical guide to the fulfillment of your dreams.* Bantam, 2009.

3. Darwin, Charles, and Oliver Francis. *On the origin of species.* Macmillan Collectors Library, 2017.

4. Feloni, Richard. "KFC founder Colonel Sanders didn't achieve his remarkable rise to success until his 60s." *Business Insider*, Business Insider, 25 June 2015, www.businessinsider.com/how-kfc-founder-colonel-sanders-achieved-success-in-his-60s-2015-6.

Chapter 5

1. Ross, Lee. "The intuitive psychologist and his shortcomings: distortions in the attribution process." *Advances in Experimental Social Psychology* , Edited by L. Berkowitz, vol. 10, 1977, pp. 173–220., doi:10.1016/s0065-2601(08)60357-3.

Chapter 6

1. D'Amore, Drew. "Social awareness as an indicator of self-awareness: the meadcooley model and research methodology in nonhuman primates." *TCNJ Journal of Student Scholarship*, Apr. 2008.

Chapter 7

1. Shilling, Dianne. "10 Steps To Effective Listening." *Forbes*, Forbes Magazine, July 2014, www.forbes.com/sites/womensmedia/2012/11/09/10-steps-to-effective-listening/.

Chapter 8

1. Collin, Catherine, et al. *The psychology book: big ideas simply explained.* DK Publishers, 2012.

2. Douglas, Karen M. "Deindividuation." *Encyclopædia Britannica*, Encyclopædia Britannica, inc., 3 Aug. 2017, www.britannica.com/topic/deindividuation.

3. Fisher, Aubrey. *Small group decision making: communication and the group process.* 2nd ed., McGraw-Hill Book, 1980.

4. Heifetz, Ronald Abadian, et al. *The practice of adaptive leadership: tools and tactics for changing your organization and the world.* Harvard Business Press, 2009.

5. Kassin, Saul, et al. *Social Psychology.* 9th ed., Cengage Learning, 2013.

Chapter 9

1. Greene, Robert. *The 48 Laws of Power.* Penguin Books, 2000.

2. Reynolds, David S. "John Wilkes Booth and the higher law: was Abraham Lincoln's assassin inspired by the militant abolitionist John Brown?" *The Atlantic*, 12 Apr. 2015, www.theatlantic.com/politics/archive/2015/04/john-wilkes-booth-and-the-higher-law/385461/.

3. The Editors of Encyclopædia Britannica. "Trojan horse." *Encyclopædia Britannica*, Encyclopædia Britannica, inc., 27 Apr. 2015, www.britannica.com/topic/Trojan-horse.

Chapter 11

1. Heifetz, Ronald A. *Leadership without easy answers.* Belknap Press, 2003.

2. Heifetz, Ronald A., and Marty Linsky. *Leadership on the line staying alive through the dangers of leading.* Harvard Business Review Press, 2002.

ABOUT THE AUTHOR

Michael Kouly began his career as a Reuters war journalist. He covered armed conflicts that involved, Israel, Lebanon, Syria, Iran, Hezbullah, Islamic extremists, terrorism, the United States, Kuwait, Iraq and others... He also covered musical concerts, fashion shows and car racing.

Writing about wars, geopolitics, international diplomacy, and global events offered Michael unique opportunities to witness, analyze and write about leadership at the highest levels: where bad leadership meant the loss of thousands of lives and good leadership led to avoiding wars, saving lives and rebuilding shattered countries.

Michael also exercised corporate leadership over a period of 30 years as he led the growth of regional and international businesses. He is a three-time CEO and president at organizations like Reuters, Orbit and Cambridge Institute for Global Leadership, managing people in more than 20 countries.

Over the span of his career, Michael made some good decisions that generated remarkable success and also some not so good decisions that offered valuable lessons on what works and what doesn't when exercising leadership - emphasizing the mindset of "you either win or learn".

From as far back as he can remember, Michael has been fascinated by leadership. He has spent his life learning about leadership, purpose and strategy by practicing them, watching others lead and by conducting extensive research on the art and science of mobilizing people and organizations towards growth and noble purposes.

Michael is a World Bank Fellow, author and keynote speaker about leadership, strategy, purpose and international politics. He is the founder of the Kouly Institute and the creator of unique Executive Leadership Programs, that have been delivered to thousands of top business executives, NGO's and government leaders worldwide.

He also dedicates time to various non-profit organizations such as the Middle East Leadership Academy (MELA), Central Eurasia Leadership Academy (CELA), South East Asia Leadership Academy (SEALA) and Leaders Across Boarders (LAB).

His calling is to help people, organizations and countries lead purpose driven lives.

Michael studied at Harvard and Princeton Universities, and is an advisor to state leaders.

Other Books By The Author

FINDING YOUR HUMMUS

This book will provide you, your colleagues, family and friends with insights about life and business to unleash your personal and organizational power.

• Shift happens in life and business, are you ready?

• What is the prime philosophy behind starting a business of growth and sustainable success?

• Do you, your people and business have a guiding purpose? This book is about finding your calling.

• Do you have a personal and organizational strategy to fulfill your purpose? This book is about self awareness, self motivation and self leadership that together can achieve self fulfillment.

• How do you deal with competition, conflict and confusion? This book is rich with empowering inspirational quotes that generate strength and lead to self actualization.

• What is the mindset to lead a life of resilience, abundance and significance? This book is about finding your passion and discovering your way of living a purpose driven life.

In The Making...
A New Title
by Michael Kouly

Made in the USA
Columbia, SC
22 June 2018